SACRED COMPLEXES OF DEOGHAR AND RAJGIR

To

My Parents

Who inspired me for higher values in life

SACRED COMPLEXES OF DEOGHAR AND RAJGIR

S. NARAYAN

CONCEPT PUBLISHING COMPANY
NEW DELHI

First Published 1983

Sachindra Narayan (*b.* 1947-

Published by

Naurang Rai
Concept Publishing Company
H-13, Bali Nagar
NEW DELHI-110015 (India)

Printed by

Patel Enterprises
at Sunil Printers
1067, Ajay Palace, Naraina
New Delhi-110 028

FOREWORD

The Anthropological Approach to the study of civilisation is a latecomer in Indian anthropology. Initiated by A.L. Krober, Ralph Linton, Robert Redfield, Milton Singer and others in the fifties it was introduced in India by Nirmal Kumar Bose, Irawati Karve and L.P. Vidyarthi. The anthropological approach to the study of civilisation is primarily based on the part-whole interactions within the civilisational frame. The anthropologists relate some elements of the Great Tradition to the life of the ordinary folk and rural people.

Since the publication of the *Sacred Complex of Hindu Gaya* (1962), the various dimensions of Indian civilisation have been studied by several scholars. During the last 20 years several studies have been undertaken which go a long way in establishing as well as refining the terms and concepts, methods and approaches to the study of Indian civilisation.

Sacred centres in India form links in a series of complex symbolic networks where each individual shrine is in a nexus of ritual activity and each such centre occupies a part in the Hindu mosaic which perpetuates and upholds a continuity in traditions that date back to antiquity. Sacred complexes play a useful role in national integration particularly in a country like India known for its linguistic and cultural diversity. Far from being isolated phenomena, temple complexes and their attendant ritual activity form part of a socio-religious matrix connecting people belonging to varying geographical regions to a common set of traditions.

Under this theoretical frame Dr. Sachindra Narayan's studies of Deoghar and Rajgir were undertaken in the early seventies and are evidently pieces of meticulous research. These sacred complexes have undergone further elaboration and attract more pilgrims, some of whom are however, tourists. A need is being felt to study these sacred complexes in terms of the sacred-secular continuum. These need to be studied and analysed in terms of rise and fall of the pilgrim centres on a comparative base and in the time perspective.

I am happy that Sachindra Narayan's studies of Deoghar and Rajgir have utilised some of the concepts and hypotheses developed in terms of the study of sacred complexes in India. These studies make a valuable contribution to cultural anthropology in enlarging upon the role of sacred complexes as agents of national integration and as helping to maintain an equilibrium between the forces of traditional and modern culture.

This volume also brings out the process of secondary urbanisation and modernisation. One of the salient hypotheses put to the test is that sacred complexes including the sacred specialists have undergone modification and transformation as the result of the overall development in the larger universe of Hindu civilisation of which they are a part.

Dr. Sachindra Narayan with his meticulous research and hard work has continued to serve the cause of Indian anthropology and has carved out a place for himself in Indian Social Science. I sincerely hope that this publication of his will find recognition in the fields of civilisational study.

Professor and Head
Department of Anthropology,
Ranchi University
RANCHI-834001

L.P. VIDYARTHI

CONTENTS

ACKNOWLEDGEMENT

I AM thankful to Prof. L.P. Vidyarthi, Prof. Sachchidananda, Prof. K.N. Sahay, Dr. A.N. Sandhwar, Dr. B.N. Saraswati, Prof. Surjit Sinha for their comments and suggestions. I am indeed obliged to Prof. Vidyarthi under whose supervision the work was done. I am also thankful to U.G.C., New Delhi for their financial support to this study. I am equally thankful to the personnel of the typing and library section of the A.N. Sinha Institute of Social Studies, Patna for their cooperation. My special thanks are due to my respondents with whose cooperation the work could be accomplished. I am also thankful to Mrs. Sova Narayan for her assistance during various stages of data collection and report writing of this work. I am thankful to Shri Naurang Rai for publishing the book in time and to Mrs. Suhasini Ramaswamy for her editorial assistance.

SACHINDRA NARAYAN

Introduction

RELIGION is one of the most important aspects of culture studied by anthropologists and other social scientists. Not only is it found in every known human society, it also significantly interacts with other cultural institutions. It finds expression in material culture, in human behaviour and in value systems, morals and ethics. It interacts with systems of family organization, marriage, economics, law and politics; it enters into the realms of medicine, science and technology; and it has inspired rebellions and wars as well as sublime works of art. No other cultural institution presents so vast a range of expression and implication. Religious concepts and ideas are not constrained by physical environment. Their formulations meet with no other limitations than those inquiring spirit of the human mind itself.

The complexity of religious phenomena and their reflection in so many other aspects of life have attracted scholars from many disciplines: historians, philosophers, psychologists, anthropologists and sociologists have analysed religion each with his own methods, with an already extensive body of literature dealing with various aspects of religion. A question may well be asked: can anthropology significantly contribute to a further understanding of religion?

A distinctive aspect of religion is that it deals with, or has reference to, the sacred. Emile Durkheim (1961:52), in formulating this distinction, maintained that everywhere man classified things into two opposing categories—the sacred and the profane. The sacred is attended by prohibitions, dispensations and prescriptions which do not usually apply to the secular elements of culture, while the profane is the everyday world, dealt with in a practical and matter-of-fact manner.

Durkheim's study of religion thus emphasizes human attitudes and behaviour. Indeed most anthropological field workers have reported that people act at times in special ways, motivated by the posited existence of culturally conceived sacred categories. The distinction is thus not spurious, but is quite difficult to handle because almost every form of human behaviour can be invested with religious meaning. Religious behaviour thus cannot be identified outside its cultural context or its religious setting. Religious attitudes and emotions are not necessarily different from any other secular attitudes and emotions. Prayer is often offered in everyday speech, it becomes religious language only when it is directed to culturally posited supernatural powers. Music, dancing and singing become sacred when they are performed to communicate with, or please, the gods. Some cultures have distinctive styles of music for religious occasions, but there is nothing in these musical modes to make them intrinsically sacred. Eating and drinking are profane activities which become religious only in a ritual setting. The criterion of the sacred, then, becomes significant only in its religious setting.

In anthropology, the shift from tribal studies to urban studies is a jump The field of urban anthropology is new, and therefore it is not surprising that anthropologists in India have not made much headway. The association of anthropologists with the Calcutta Metropolitan Planning organization has been of long standing. The late Nirmal Kumar Bose brought his knowledge of geography and anthropology to bear upon the study of Calcutta (61). Vidyarthi has posited the idea of the sacred complex in the study of the priest community in a city in Bihar. Several American and Indian anthropologists have been involved in the study of the sacred complex of Bhubaneshwar and Puri under the leadership of Cora Du Bois. B.N. Saraswati has been engaged in a long-term and multidirectional study of the holy city of Varanasi. These studies are going to break new ground. Work in these areas may produce notable contributions by India to the science of anthropology.

A full-length study of the sacred city of Gaya as a dimension of Indian civilization in the framework of Redfield's and Singer's theories has been attempted by Vidyarthi (1961). It is an aid to the undertaking of religion in India in terms of the great traditional life of the communities.

The study of Indian civilization in relation to the sacred complexes received considerable emphasis during the period under review. On the model of the study of sacred complex of Gaya by Vidyarthi, field researches were undertaken in many places of pilgrimage both in north and south India and a few papers and books have been published among which mention may be made of Rajgir (Narayan, 1969), Deoghar (Narayan, 1971), Janakpur (Jha, 1971), Bhubaneshwar (Mahapatra, 1972), Bodh Gaya (Narayan, 1978), Kashi (Vidyarthi and Saraswati, 1978) and a general survey of the temples dedicated to the deities of Shiva, Vaishnava and of the Shakta cult (Goswami and Morab, 1970). A seminar on the sacred complex in India was jointly organised by the I.C.S.S.R. and Department of Anthropology, Ranchi University, in 1973. The Seminar discussed at length the substantive data on places of pilgrimage specially collected from Varanasi and analysed the various theoretical implications of sacred complex studies. These papers along with the summary of the discussion have been published in a book form.

On a wider frame, the study of religion, specially Hinduism, in a context with the understanding of Indian civilization has attracted the attention of Chicago School of Anthropologists. The penetrative analysis of the Indian social structure made in the edited volume by Milton Singer and B .S. Cohan was followed up by these scholars. Cohan published a book entitled *India: The Social Anthropology of a Civilization* in the Anthropology of Modern Societies Series in 1971. The book presents a bird's eye view of Indian civilization. In such an appraisal of continuity and change as a constant factor in the history of Indian civilization Cohan has made a penetrating analysis of the geographical, demographic, historical, social and structural aspects of Indian civilization and has clearly brought out the role of Hinduism and other minor religions in building up Indian civilization.

The study of religion as practised in the different parts of India has been one of the chief focii of Indian anthropology. If a number of scholars like Milton Singer, M.N. Srinivas, L P. Vidyarthi and his students like B.N. Saraswati, S. Narayan, M. Jha, etc. have studied religion and the sacred complexes as a dimension of Indian civilization, others like P.K. Bhowmick, D.N. Majumdar, T.R. Singh have described the changing religious institutions of certain communities, and the census operations have made a statistical, factual appraisal of the fairs and festivals of the different States. All these approaches have fruitfully contributed to the store of knowledge of Indian religion. There is need, however, to take up the studies of religious beliefs and practices as reflected in the ancient texts and religious scriptures. These are full of social facts and deserve to be studied anthropologically and contextually. It is hoped that in the process of Indianisation of social research both the textual and contextual approaches to the study of religion will be integrated, and as such an integrated approach is likely to be of considerable significance in understanding Indian civilization and culture.

Deoghar, the sacred city of Baidyanathdham, was studied to test a few hypotheses which may be stated as follows :

1. The sacred complex is a uniting agent which brings the people of different classes, castes, etc., on a common saddle and develops national integration.
2. The sacred complex is a balancing force between the traditional and modern culture.
3. The sacred specialist of a Hindu place of pilgrimage maintains a distinct style of life and transmits certain elements of the great tradition to the rural population of India by popularising certain texts, by organizing pilgrimages and by officiating as the ritual and temple priests.
4. The sacred complex in general and the sacred specialists in particular have been in the process of modification and transformation as a result of the general developments in the larger universe of Hindu civilization of which they are a part.

My earlier study of the sacred complex of Rajgir, which forms Part II of this volume, developed interest in me, and some of these hypotheses were also tested there. My study of Rajgir also encouraged me to undertake such studies further, and, consequently I studied Deoghar, Varanasi and Bodh Gaya. Rajgir and Deoghar are being published here in one volume.

Deoghar is about 226 km east of Patna and 330 km west of Calcutta. Jasidih, the nearest and one of the important railway junctions of the Eastern Railway, is connected with Baidyanathdham by a shuttle train. Baidyanathdham is 7 km from Jasidih which can be reached by a parallel metalled road also.

The historical account of Baidyanathdham was little known prior to the travel account of the Chinese pilgrim Hieun-Tsiang who visited India about A.D. 645. There is a mention of the land and people of this tract and of the shrine of Lord Baidyanath at Deoghar in the Bhavishyat Puran which was compiled in the 15th or 16th century A.D.[1] Malik Ikhtiaruddin Bin Bukhtiar Khilji made Deoghar his capital in A.D. 1201 which was then known as Deogarh[2]. Baidyanathdham is also known as Deoghar which is being treated as a town since 1901 and now is a sub-divisional town.

According to the Shiva Puran,[3] it was in the Tretayug and according to Hindu belief that the demon Ravan, the king of Lanka, convinced that his capital could not be perfect without the presence of Mahadeva, went to Kailash and requested Him to make Lanka his permanent home. Mahadeva did not grant this prayer but told Ravan that one of the twelve emblems of this divinity (Jyotirlingams) would quite serve the purpose and that he might take one but on condition that the transfer should be effected without a break in the journey, since should the Lingam be deposited anywhere on the earth in the course of the journey it would remain fixed on that spot forever. Ravan, thereupon, took the Lingam and began his journey back to Lanka. The gods dreaded the effect of the Lingam being established in the kingdom of their most powerful enemy; for, if Mahadeva were to be the protector of the demon's metropolis they could never overthrow him. They, accordingly, sat in a solemn conclave and devised a plan for outwitting Ravan. Varuna, the regent of water, entered the bladder of Ravan, with the result that the demon had to descend to earth to relieve himself. Then Vishnu in the garb of an old Brahman appeared before Ravan and began to converse with him. Unconscious of the plot, Ravan begged of the Brahman to help him by holding the sacred emblem for a few minutes, a request which was readily acceded to. Ravan then handed over the Lingam to him and retired to ease himself. On return he found the Brahman had disappeared and the Lingam was lying on the ground at a considerable distance from the place where he had descended on earth. Ravan tried hard to lift the Lingam but in vain. Growing desperate he used force and succeeded only in breaking a piece of the top of the Lingam. Realising his folly, he prostrated himself before the Lingam and begged for pardon. Further, to atone for his sacrilege he came back to the place and worshipped the divinity with libations of sacred water brought from the source of the Ganges. (This was afterwards rendered superfluous by the digging of a well, in which the waters of all the sacred rivers were stored). The spot where Ravan came down is believed to be the present Harlajori and the place where the Lingam was deposited is believed to be the present Baidyanatheshwar's temple.

According to the Padma Puran the Brahman with whom Ravan entrusted the Lingam deposited it in due form, consecrated it with water from a neighbouring tank, offered his prayers and then departed. A Bhil who was an eyewitness to this received instruction from the Brahman as to how the worship of the emblem should be conducted but, having no utensil at hand, brought the water required for the libation in his mouth. When Ravan finally returned to the spot the Bhil narrated all that had happened and pointed out that the Brahman was none other than Vishnu Himself. Ravan by virtue of his powers, then bore a well with an arrow and brought into it the waters of all the sacred pools on earth for a fitting worship of the God Mahadeva.

According to another tradition (myth) not referred to in any Puran, the Lingam lay neglected after the death of Ravan until it was noticed by a rude hunter, Baiju by name, who accepted it as his God and worshipped the deity daily proclaiming it to the world as the Lord of Baiju (Baidyanath). Earlier the Lingam was known by its original name of Jyotirlingam (the Lingam of light) or by the name it derived from its transfer, namely, Ravaneshwar.

Sir William Hunter in the Annals of Rural Bengal[4] relates the Santhal tradition of Baidyanathdham as follows:[5] "In olden times a band of Brahmans settled on the banks of the beautiful highland lake beside which the holy city stands. Around there was only forest and mountains, in which dwelt the black races. The Brahmans placed the symbol of their God Siva near the lake and did sacrifice to it, but came as before to the three great stones which their fathers had worshipped, and which are to be seen at the western entrance of the holy city to this day. The Brahmans moreover ploughed the land and brought water from the lake to nourish the soil, but the hillmen hunted and fished as of old or tended their herds . . . . But in process of time the Brahmans, finding the land good, became slothful giving themselves up to lust and seldom calling on their God Shiva. Thus the black tribes, who came to worship the great stones, saw and wondered at it more and more, till at last one of them by name Baiju, a man of mighty arm and rich in all sorts of cattle, became wrathful at the lies and wantonness of the Brahmans and vowed he would beat the symbol of their God, Shiva, with his club every day before touching any food. This he did but one morning his cattle strayed into the forest and after seeking them all day he came home hungry and weary and having hastily bathed in the lake sat down to his supper. Just as he stretched out his hand to take the food he called to mind his vow and worn out as he was, he got up, limped painfully to the Brahmans' idol on the margin of the lake and beat it with his club. Then suddenly a splendid form sparkling with jewels rose from the water and said 'Behold the man who forgets his hunger and his weariness to beat me while my priests sleep with their concubines at home and neither give me to eat nor to drink. Let him ask of me what he will and it shall be given.' Then Baiju answered, I am strong of arm and rich of cattle. I am leader of my people, what want I more? Thou art called Nath (Lord) and let me be called Nath and let thy temple go by this name. "Amen", replied the deity. Henceforth the temple was known as Baidyanath temple."

There are other stories also in the Purans explaining the origin and *mahatam* of the deity enshrined at Deoghar. It has been said in the Shiva Puran that unable to bear the disrespect shown to her husband Shiva by her father Daksha, Sati committed suicide. This plunged the Lord in great grief and, in a fit of frenzy, He plunged His Trident into the body of Sati and began roaming with Her body till Vishnu cut the body with his discus (*Chakra*) into fiftytwo parts, one of which, the heart, fell at Deoghar and thus it is also known as Hridyapeeth (Land of the heart) or Chitabhumi (Burial Place).

Basukinath, physically separated from Deoghar but closely associated with Baidyanathdham on mythological level, has also been included in this study. It has been described as "village" in the District Census Handbook (Santhal Parganas) and further described as the place. ". . . Famous for the temple of Lord Shiva which is considered to be very holy and powerful by the Hindus. The temple is about 150 years old and is said to have been built by Basuki a Harijan. . . ." According to a legend it is one of the Jyotirlingams but it has not been referred to in the Shiva Puran. The place was full of forest. A demon known as Daruk was dwelling in the forest and the forest was known after his name, that is, Darukavan. Once, one Supriya Vaishya, who was passing through the forest, was caught by the demon. Supriya called upon Lord Shiva to rescue her. Thus it was made one of His permanent abodes on the request of the devout. Yet another popular legend is that once there was a famine and the people were migrating in search of food. Darukvan was full of edibles. A band of people settled here. Basu was one of them. Once his tool touched the Shivalingam while digging the roots and profuse bleeding started. Basu became anxious. He heard the voice of Shiva saying that he should worship Him regularly and the place henceforth would be known after his name, that is, Basukinath.

II

Rajgir, city of historical and religious importance, is situated in the Silao Police Station of Bihar Sub-division of Nalanda district. It is located 90 km south-east of Patna (capital of Bihar) and 60 km north-east of Gaya (a religious city). According to the 1961 Census the total population of Rajgir was 9,033. Rajgir town is spread over an area of 5 sq km. It is a developing township. The people in general are simple and kind. Generally the male folk don a simple dhoti and kurta and women wear a saree and blouse. A few of them, of course young, can be seen in fashionable dresses. Currently, the growing township is gaining popularity due to Buddhism and Jainism.

The history of the city is quite glorious. It was the capital of Magadh and was known by more than one name of which mention may be made of Vasumati, Brahdrathapura, Grivaraja, Kusagrapura and Rajgriha. The name of Vasumati is found in the Ramayana, probably it owes its origin to the mythical king Vasu, son of Brahma, to whom the foundation of the city is traditionally ascribed. The name of Brahdrathapura is reminiscent of King Brahadratha, a forefather of the famous king Jarasandh and the progenitor of a dynasty. The physical condition of the area comprising the city, viz. the hills encircling it on all sides, have given it the name of Grivaraja, the enclosure of hills. The name Kusagrapura is found in the literature of Hieun Tsiang and of the Jains and in some Sanskrit or Buddhist texts. Hieun-Tsiang says that it means the city of superior grass and has reference to the fragrant grass growing all round in the city and owes its origin to King Kusagra, the successor of Brahadratha. The name Rajgriha or royal abode is an appropriate designation of a place that remained the capital of Magadh for centuries. Hieun-Tsiang, however, implies that this name was strictly applicable only to the New Rajgriha to the north of hill area. The hills that encircle Rajgriha are traditionally five in number. Their enumeration differs in different texts. The Mahabharata, for example, gives their name as Vaibhara, Varaha, Vrishabha, Rishigiri and Chityaka; at another place, however, the text specifies them as Pondara, Vipula, Varakaka, Chityaka and Matanga. The Pali texts have another set of names, Vaibhara, Pondara, Vipula, Gridhkuta and Rishigiri. The present names are Vaibhara, Vipula, Ratna, Chatta, Saita, Udaya, Girdhkutta and Sona, their origin being due to Jainas. It is very difficult to identify the modern names with their ancient representation.

It is stated in the Ramayana that Grivaraja was founded by Vasu, the fourth son of Brahma, the Creator. For a long time after this tradition is silent about the city till we come to the days of the Kurukshetra War, when Brahadratha, it is said, established himself at this place and became the progenitor of the Brahadratha dynasty known after his name. One of his successors was the famous Jarasandh who is said to have gained a reputation as the most powerful king of his time. He had a matrimonial alliance with Kamsa, the ruler of Mathura and maternal uncle of Lord Krishna. When Krishna killed Kamsa for his misdeeds, Jarasandh marched on Mathura to exterminate the clansmen of Krishna but was repulsed. After this Krishna visited Grivaraja with the Pandava brothers

Bhima and Arjuna and, acting on his advice, Bhima killed Jarasandh in a duel. The dynasty of Jarasandh, however, continued to rule till later times.

Coming to more historical times when the Buddha was practising his law he found a new dynasty with Bimbisara as the king (543-491 B.C.) ruling over Magadh. He was one of the powerful kings ruling over northern India. The other three being Prasenjit of Kosala, Udyana of Vatsa and Pradyota of Avanti. Bimbisara though different in lineage was at least equal to the others in prowess and extent of kingdom. He committed Magadha to a career of conquest. The centripetal forces that began to operate under him stopped only at the time of Ashoka, when Magadha became the centre of an empire extending over most of India and Afghanistan.

Bimbisara was a great admirer of the Buddha and his creed. In his old age he is said to have been imprisoned and killed by his son Ajatasatru (491-459 B.C.), who, however, later submitted to the Buddha and became a convert to his creed. Fahien, the Chinese pilgrim, ascribes to him the foundation of new Rajgriha outside the hills and is partially supported by Hieun Tsiang. In the Pali text he is said to have repaired the fortifications of the city in anticipation of an attack from the ferocious Pradyota, the king of Avanti.

Rajgriha was an important centre of Buddhism and the Buddha himself passed many years of his "ministration" at this place. It was the scene of many sermons and important events of his life. He lived in the different localities of the city, but his favourite resort was Gridharkuta or the vulture's peak. He admired the city and its environments and his impression is summed up in his own words as given in the Pali text :

> Delightful is Rajgriha, delightful is Gridharkuta, delightful is Gautama-nyagrodha, delightful is the Saptparni cave on the side of Vasibhra, delightful is Kasia on the Rishigiri side, delightful is Sonpa-Saundika-Praghbara in Sitavana, delightful is the Tapodarma, delightful is Kalandaka lake in Venuvan, delightful is the mango grove of Jivaka,"...

After the attainment of Nirvana by the Buddha, Ajatasatru brought the corporeal body of Lord Buddha to Rajgir and enshrined it inside stupa. A few months later when the leading Buddhist monks decided to hold a council to form a corpus of teachings of the Buddha, Ajatasatru accommodated them in a large hall in front of tbe Saptparni cave, specially built for the purpose.

The modern religious importance of the place is largely due to Buddhism and Jainism which, with a characteristic fondness for heights, have built temples at the tops of almost all the hills. These temples throughout laying claim to antiquity attract pilgrims from the distant parts of India.

Rajgir is important for Muslims also because Hazrat Mukhdum Shah Sharfuddin Ahmed Yalia of Maner, the King of Salikas (a class of Faqirs) has made a special *chilla* on the hill in the town of Rajgir which may be described as the particular place of God. There is an *Idgah* (monument) just near to the Laxmi Narayan Temple where they offer *Namaz* (prayers) during Id.

Rajgir was under the zamindari of Nawab of Hussainbad till the abolition of this system.

There are some folk shrines also in Rajgir where only local people worship.

III

The first section of the book discusses Deoghar and the second is about Rajgir. The quantum of data is not uniform since the work was carried at two varying levels. Both the sacred complexes of Rajgir and Deoghar have been discussed broadly under three analytical concepts that is sacred geography, sacred specialists and sacred performances, followed by a conclusion.

REFERENCES

1. *District Census Hand Book* (Santhal Parganas), 1961.
2. Ibid.
3. Chaturth Koti Rudra Sanhita of the Shiva Puran.
4. *District Census Hand Book* (Santhal Parganas), 1961, pp. XX.
5. Ibid.

PART ONE

DEOGHAR

Sacred Geography

1

DEOGHAR, popularly known as Baidyanathdham, is located in the demographically tribal dominated district of Dumka in Bihar State. It is 226 km. east of Patna and covers an area of 6.29 sq. miles and with a population of about 45,000 (Municipal records, 1961). At present there are two degree colleges, eight high schools, a Hindu Vidyapeeth, cinema halls, factories, subdivisional courts, market centres, etc.

The origin of Baidyanathdham is lost in the antiquity. It has been referred as Haritakivan, Ketakivan, etc., in Sanskrit texts. The name Deoghar seems to be of recent origin and probably dates from the erection of the great temple of Lord Baidyanath. It stems from Devagriha the abode of God. Although the name of the builder of the temple is not traceable, certain parts of the front portion of the temple are said to have been built by Puran Mal, an ancestor of the Maharaja of Giddhour, in 1596. So far twenty-six sacred centres have been constructed by different pilgrims, citizens and Pandas of Deoghar. Ninetyfive sacred centres were found during 1969-71.

There are both sacred and secular elements in the landscape of Deoghar. What is interesting in the settlement pattern of Deoghar is that the sacred and secular elements occupy more or less distinct areas. On the basis of the predominance of these elements the township of Deoghar may be divided into sacred and secular zones. The boundaries of the sacred zone, however, cut across the municipal limits of Deoghar town. In other words, the boundaries of the sacred zone override the boundaries of the secular zone. For our purpose the sacred complex in Deoghar covers an area of twentynine miles comprising Basukinath.

Only a few of the sacred shrines like Baidyanatheshwar,

Harlajori and Chandrakup have a reference in the Shiva Puran. Besides such textual description of the sacred centres there is an old tradition regarding the sacred boundary which is marked by a pilgrimage route, usually followed by the Kanwar[1] pilgrims. Kanwar pilgrims begin their first ritual at Sultanganj from where the Ganges water is collected for the entire pilgrimage of Deoghar. This obviously indicates that, in practice, the sacred area begins from here. After offering the holy Ganges water to Baidyanath at Deoghar, a few pilgrims proceed with the rest of the Ganges water to Basukinath where the pilgrimage is concluded. Thus contextually the sacred area of Deoghar may be considered as an area extending from Sultanganj to Basukinath. However, all pilgrims do not necessarily take to Kanwar pilgrimage.

Regarding the anthropological approach to the demarcation of the sacred zone, we have already made a reference to Vidyarthi's work which says that when two or more segments form a continuous zone it is termed as a sacred zone (Vidyarthi, 1961:5). The sacred zone of Deoghar follows this pattern. It, however, marks a departure from the sacred zone of Gaya in respect of its two distinct clusterings of sacred shrines widely spread over in space. The sacred complex of Basukinath is located at a distance of twentynine miles from Deoghar—the main shrine. Thus Deoghar and Basukinath are widely separated in space, although the two sacred places of pilgrimage form a single sacred unit so far as their sacred mythology is concerned. Indeed, the complex of Baidyanatheshwar Kshetra is divided into two subzones, i.e. Baidyanath and Basukinath. Both subzones are developing their sacred complex distinctly in a widely separated space. That they cannot be culturally separated as two distinct sacred zones is mainly because of mythological unity and the pattern of pilgrimage. Pilgrims visiting Basukinath necessarily have to come to Baidyanathdham, but all those who make a pilgrimage to Baidyanathdham do not go to Basukinath. Therefore, technically, Basukinath is a place of pilgrimage largely dependent on Baidyanathdham. The small town of Basukinath which is gradually growing in its sacred and secular element remains a sub-zone of the Baidyanatheshwar sacred zone within these two sub-zones; the sacred centres may be grouped according to their physical location as well as mythological unity between different shrines, for instance, the sacred shrines of Harlajori, Ravankunda and Shivaganga are linked with one another by the myth of Ravan. These shrines are also located in a compact area. Therefore, we may consider them as a segment of the Baidyanath sacred sub-zone. Another segment of this subzone is represented by the main shrine of Baidyanathjee surrounded by the residential buildings of the sacred specialists. The third segment, Rohini, is located at a distance of 6 km from Deoghar. It is popularly known as *Sasural* (in-law's place) of the presiding deity, that is, Baidyanath, marked by the shrine of Baidyanath, Parvatee, Nandini, Lakshmi, Vishnu and Hanuman. There is also a hermitage of a saint called Paglababa. The fourth segment located at a distance of 15 km known as Tapovan (forest for penance) is also connected with the myth of Baidyanath, but the current importance of the place is due to the Ashram of Balanand Brahmachari. Trikuti can be similarly considered as a segment of the Basukinath sacred subzone due to its mythical connection with the origin of Basukinath. The legend described elsewhere shows that Trikutinath is located at a distance of 10 km from Basukinath and forms a distinct cluster of sacred shrines. Therefore, Basukinath and Trikutinath may be regarded as two separate segments.

Within these segments there are clusters of shrines and the residential buildings of the sacred specialists. The number of clusters varies from one segment to another. The basis of clustering the shrines is its legendary unity and location helping the pilgrims in performing rituals in a single phase. Clustering of shrines may also be done on the basis of the dominance of a particular deity or a particular ritual, i.e., offering of Maur. The sacred centre is the smallest unit in the whole sacred complex (Vidyarthi, 1961:5). The plan of the sacred Kshetra of Baidyanatheswar will indicate the location and arrangement of sacred subzones, sacred segments, sacred clusters and sacred centres. We may now give a brief introduction of these places showing their sacred myths. (see Table 1.1).

TABLE 1.1 : **Sacred Places show their Sacred myths**

A Sacred sub-zone	B Segments	C Clusters	D Centres
Deoghar	Baidyanath	(A) Baidyanathjee	Ravaneshwar Baidyanath
			Parvatee
			Basha
			Laxmi Narain
			Nilkanth
			Jagat Janani
			Ganesh
			Brahma
			Gyetri
			Mahakal Vairab
			Hanuman
			Mansa
			Saraswati
			Surya
			Bagla
			Ram-Laxman-Janki
			Ganga-Jamuna-Sarswati
			Anand Vairab
			Gaurishankar
			Narmadeshwar Mahadeo
			Tara
			Kali
			Annapurna
			Keshkund
			Neerkund
			Chandrakup
		(B) Baiju Sitla	Baiju (New)
			Baiju (Old)
			Sitla
			Phagdoor
			Rammandir
		(C) Shiva Ganga —Nath Bari	Shivaganga
			Shiva
			Jagarnath
			Nath Bari
	Harlajori	(A) Harlajori Ravankund	Mansa
			Banyan
			Pipal
			Hariajori
			Ravankund
		(B) Jagarnath Mansingh	Jagarnath
			Shivalaya

A	B	C	D
			Ram
			Pipal
			Hanuman/Mansingh
	Rohini	(A) Satsang-Pagla baba Ashram	Satsang
			Sitaram
			Shiva
			Hanuman
		(B) Rohini-Kailash	Shiva
			Parvatee
			Basha
			Laxmi Narain
			Kailash
			Shiva
			Parvatee
			Nandini
	Tapovan	(A) Deosangh-Balanand	Deosangh
			Kalimandir
			Balanand Ashram
			Sphetic syambhulinga
			Kali
			Shiva
			Jagrannath
			Hanuman
			Yugalmurti
		(B) Hanthi-Pahar Kundeshwari	Hanthi Pahar
			Shiva
			Hanuman
			Kundeshwari Devi
			Shiva
			Radhakrishna
		(C) Tapovan-Shivakund	Shivakund
			Tapovan
			Shiva
			Kali Devi
			Hanuman
			Balanand Ashram
			Manokamna Devi
Basukinath	Trikuti	(A) Trikuti-Parvatee	Trikuti
			Trikuteshwar
			Parvatee
		(B) Ganesh Durga	Ganesh
			Bhairab
			Annapurna
			Durga

A	B	C	D
	Basukinath	(A) Kalimandir-Basukinath	Kalimandir
			Bhagwati Mandir
			Basukinath
			Parvatee
			Kali
			Yup
			Haranggriha
			Chandrakupa
			Laxmi
			Taramaie
			Radha Krishna
			Annapurna
			Chchinmostika
			Baglamukt ki
			Panchdeota
		(B) Shivaganga —Tara	Pipal
			Banyan
			Tara

There are four sacred segments in the sacred geography of the Deoghar subzones. The first three segments are united with one another through a single myth of Ravan (referred to earlier in detail) though widely spread over in the space. The sacred centres of the fourth segment are also linked with one another through a single myth of Basukinath (referred to earlier in detail).

The sacred geography of Deoghar can also be classified on the basis of Kanwar pilgrimage. (For details see Chapter Six).

The sacred centres of the Baidyanath segment are of central importance owing to Baidyanathjee. Baidyanath temple is centrally situated at Baidyanathdham. Twentysix sacred centres are located in this segment. The Baidyanath sacred centre is the oldest centre of the segment. The Shivalingam at Baidyanathjee does not resemble any other lingam found at any place of pilgrimage to the best knowledge of the writer. The lingam is flat and curved. The dotted line on the left side of the curved lingam is supposed to be the emblem of Parvatee. Thus it is considered that by worshipping Baidyanath only one worships both Baidyanath and Parvatee.

Basaha, the carrier of Baidyanath, is located in front of Baidyanath temple and is worshipped by the pilgrims. Other sacred centres enshrine the deity of its name. These centres have been constructed in the course of time by different sardar Pandas (chief sacred specialists) and Pandas (sacred specialists).

Kesh Kund is 3 ft in diameter and 6 inches deep. Mundan ceremonies are performed here. The holy water offered to Baidyanath is collected in a sacred kund called Neerkund. Chandrakupa is the mythological well constructed by the legendary hero, Ravan.

The Baiju-Sitla is one of the clusters of Baidyanath segment. Baiju Sitla sacred centre finds reference in the Shiva Puran.[2] Textually, Baidyanath, pleased with Baiju, had granted that his name would be taken before His, ie. Baiju+Nath=Baidyanath (Lord of Baiju). A Shivalingam in blackstone is enshrined here. The centre is under the custody of a woman of the Dhanuk caste. Another sacred centre located nearby is that of Sitla. Sitla is one of the goddesses. She is represented here by a cemented lump and vermillion. On every Tuesday women from every Panda family come here for weekly sacred performances with vermillion, flowers, water, milk and incense. Phagdoor, another sacred centre of this cluster, is about a furlong ahead on the right of the Sitla sacred centre. It is also known as Dolmunkh. It is a neglected centre. During the Holi festival a craddle is kept within the centre in which Krishna is shown playing Holi with Baidyanath. Holi was generally celebrated by the late Sardar Panda, now it is celebrated by the Purohit of Sardar Panda. The Ram sacred centre of this cluster is mythologically not linked with rest of the centres of this cluster. The local population has constructed it to fill the gap created by the absence of any centre of Ram in the Baidyanath Kshetra. The centre enshrines a marble idol of Sita, Ram, Laxman and Hanuman.

Shivaganga is a sacred tank of the Shivaganga Nathbari sacred cluster. Mythologically, Ravan wanted to cleanse himself after easing, but he could not find any tank or well. So he fisted the earth and created the Shivaganga. Pilgrims bathe here before worshipping Baidyanath. Shiva temple is at the main gate of Shivaganga. It enshrines a Shivalingam where pilgrims offer holy water after bathing in the Shivaganga. Jagarnath temple is one of the sacred centres of this cluster. It enshrines marble idol of Lord Krishna and Radha. Nathbari, a centre of Nath Sampradaya (Sect) of this cluster is dilapidated and in condition of neglect.

There are two clusters in the Harlajori segment. The two sacred centres, Harlajori and Ravankund, of this segment are mythologically linked with each other. Harlajori enshrines the idol of Shiva and Parvatee. It has a mythical relationship with Baidyanath. There are six sacred centres in the Jagarnath Mansingh cluster. Jagarnath centre enshrines an idol of Jagarnath. Close to it is a Shivalaya enshrining the Shivalingam, popularly believed to be one of the manifestations of Baidyanath. Close to it is a Ram mandir having an idol of Ram, Sita and Laxman and close to it is a Hanuman sacred centre. Hanuman is being represented here by an engraved idol. Close to it is a pipal tree where devotees offer jal, gur, til, paisa, phool, prasad and dhoop on Saturdays.

Satsang

Paglababa Ashram and Rohini Kailas have the two clusters of the Rohini segment. Sri Sri Thakur Anukul Chandra established the Satsang Ashram on 2 September, 1946. It was originally started at Pabna (Bangladesh) in 1925. There is only a portrait of the Thakur in the middle of the Satsang premises where Ashramites observe daily sacred performances. Thakur himself observed sacred performances at the Baidyanath sacred centre.

Sriniwasangan is commonly known as Paglababa Ashram. Sri Sri Lilanand Thakur established it on 20 February 1967, and dedicated it to Krishna and Shiva. Shiva is represented in his usual form whereas Krishna, Ram, Sita and Hanuman are represented by silver idols.

There are eight sacred centres in the Rohini Kailash sacred cluster. Rohini is believed to be the *Sasural* (in-law's place) of Baidyanath. Here Shiva is represented in his usual form and Parvatee by a silver idol. Basha, the carrier of Shiva, is represented in stone. Close to it is the centre of Laxmi and Narain who are represented by marble idols. Nandini, the cow of Shiva, is also represented by a stone cow. Deosangh-Balanand, Hanthi Pahar-Kundeshwari and Tapovan-Shivakund are the three clusters of the Tapovan sacred segment. Mythologically this segment is not associated with the first three segments.

Most of the sacred centres of this segment are of recent origin.

Deosangh is an Ashram of Deosangh Balanand cluster, popularly known as Nav Durga mandir. Swami Narendra Brahmachari established it in September, 1955. The Ashram dedicated to Baglodevi, also houses Shiva in His usual form and Parvatee, Vishnu and Laxmi in the form of marble idols. The ashram is decorated with full size oil paintings of different gods and goddesses. It is believed that once Devi came in the dream of Swami Narendra Brahmachari and ordered him to establish an ashram at this place. So the Ashram is the fulfilment of Her desire. Kalimandir is another sacred centre of this cluster. An idol of Kali and Shiva lingam are enshrined here. Local priests are the custodians of this centre.

Balanand Brahmachari Ashram was established in 1906. Katyayain built a commemorative temple dedicated to Baleshwar Mahadeva along with a Yagnasala. This formed the nucleus of the Ashram named Ramnivas Brahmacharya Ashram after Ramcharan Basu, and is popularly known as Balanand Ashram. Another cluster of this segment is the Hanthi Pahar-Kundeshwari. Hanthi Pahar is two miles south east from Deoghar tower. The structure of the tiny hillock is similar to that of an elephant, hence it is commonly known as Hanthi Pahar. Shrines of different gods and goddesses have been erected here by local businessmen in the last fifty years. The Kundeshwari sacred centre also comes under this cluster. Rampada Bandhopadhyaya constructed the temple of Durga at Kunda village. This is why it is popularly known as Kundeshwari Devika mandir. The last cluster of the Tapovan sacred segment is the Tapovan-Shivakunda. Except a sacred tank popularly known as Shivakund all sacred centres are situated on the Tapovan hill. It is a small hillock about 9 km south east of Deoghar. There is a cave at the top of the hillock and, mythologically, Ravan did meditation in this cave.

Trikuti-Parvatee, Ganesh-Durga, Kalimandir-Basukinath and Shivaganga-Tara are the clusters, of the Basukinath sacred subzone of the sacred geography of Deoghar. Trikuti is 17 km from Deoghar on the Dumka road. It is 2,470 feet above sea level. Trikuti, the second highest hill of Bihar, is famous for Trikuteshwarnath temple. Trikuteshwar, Parvatee, Bhairab,

Annapurna and Durga are housed at the top of the hill in their usual form.

Basukinath is 39 km from Deoghar on the Dumka road. It is believed that Basukinath is one of the Dwadas Yotirlingams but it has not been referred to in any text. According to a popular myth the place was a huge forest. Once a Supriya Vaisya was passing through the forest and was arrested by a demon. On a request, Shiva rescued her. Supriya then requested Shiva to make the forest his abode along with Parvatee. According to another legend there was a famine. People were migrating in search of food. Daruk forest was full of edibles. So some came and settled here. Once, while digging for edible roots, Basu's foot touched Shiva and bleeding started. Basu became anxious. He heard the voice of Shiva asking him to worship the Lingam. Pleased He gave him a boon that henceforth the place would be known after the name of Basuki. Thus, from that very day the place is known as Basukinath. Basukinath is represented through the usual Shivalingam. The Lingam is tied with a flat piece of silver in the belief that it was broken by Basu while digging for edibles. Most of the sacred centres of Basukinath are similar to the sacred centre of Baidyanath. There are fifteen sacred centres in the Kalimandir-Basukinath cluster. Among these Bhagwati and Kali are located on the outskirts of Basukinath and the local devotees observe sacred performance at these two centres. Both the deities are represented by cemented lumps and are non-vegetarian.

The sacred centre of the Parvatee, represented by a piece of white marble, is in front of Basukinath sacred centres. Kalimaie, Hawangriha, Chandrakupa, Taramaie, Radha-Krishna, Annapurna, Chhinmestika, Baglamukhi and Panchdeota are all located systematically one after another in a clockwise fashion. Shivaganga is located at a considerable distance from Basukinath in the extreme south corner. It is sacred where usually pilgrims bathe before worshipping Basukinath.

The sacred geography of Deoghar has been described on the basis of various religious spots which constitute from the smallest to the largest unit of worship. As stated earlier, the smallest unit of worship has been termed as sacred centre (Vidyarthi, 1961:5) which represents a single spot where a sacred performance takes place. While a number of sacred centres in and around the main sacred centre has been termed as sacred cluster. Thus we find that at Deoghar, Baidyanath is such a sacred cluster of a number of sacred centres devoted to Shiva, Parvatee, Vishnu, Laxmi, Kali, Kalvairab, Anand Vairab, Ram, Sita, Chandrakupa, Nilkanth, Jagat Janani, Ganesh, Brahma, Gayetri, Hanuman, Mansa, Surya, Bagla, Tara and Annapurna. Similarly, other segments have been described.

It has been observed that the form of worship is modified according to the dominant sacred centre of the cluster. But there are a few exceptions, for example at Baidyanath cluster where the form of worship should have been modified by Shiva owing to its dominance but a good number of goats are offered within the premises at different sacred centres every year.

When two or more clusters form a continuous segment it has been termed as "sacred segment" (Vidyarthi, 1961:5). At this organisational level different sacred centres around Baidyanath form a cluster and the Baidyanath, Baiju Sitla and Shivaganga, Nathbari clusters form a segment. The other segments have been described at great length in the preceding pages. When we look at the segmental level we find that the gods and goddesses of different seats are represented in a single cluster, e.g. Baidyanath cluster. The gods and goddesses of Shiva, Shakta and Vaishnava sects are found in the Baidyanath cluster. Vegetarian and non-vegetarian deities are also found in this cluster. In some cases all the sacred centres of a segment are vegetarian, i.e. the sacred centres of Harlajori. The sacred centres of a segment may be Brahman or non-Brahman or both. In one segment we also find that a centre is owned by an individual or by the community. In the Baidyanath segment the sacred centres of the Baidyanath cluster are owned by the community whereas the Sitla and Baiju sacred centres of the Baiju Sitla cluster are owned by individuals. The sacred specialists associated with different sacred centres of a segment may be Brahmin or non-Brahmin or both. In some cases the sacred centres of the entire cluster are managed by non-Brahmins. We find heterogeneity among the sacred specialists of a sacred cluster but even then they are homogeneous in their profession irrespective of the caste and creed and receive *daxina* from their *Jajmans*. (For details see Chapter four).

When the order of worship is taken into consideration we find that in all temples and ashrams Baidyanath in the form of Shivalingam is worshipped first.

An attempt so far, has been made to examine the sacred geography of Deoghar mainly on a synchronic level which can help us in understanding the process of growth and elaboration of sacred centres in a place of pilgrimage. This also reveals the expansion and scope of the sacred centres ranging from household and local level to the entire Hindu universe. In such a process of religious integration Vidyarthi (1961) opines, "we note the factors of combination and compromise between various symbols, sects, traditions and priesthood."

REFERENCES

1. Kanwar offering is an important ritual which is perhaps performed only in Baidyanathdham. Kanwar is made of bamboo and basket or rope in which *Gangajal* is stored at Sultanganj 90 miles away from Deoghar. The stored water is offered to Lord Baidyanath or to Basukinath for the fulfilment of maundane desires. *Deshwal* and *Marwari* pilgrims offer different kinds of Kanwar in the month of Magh and Shrawan. The entire distance is covered on foot and several purificatory rules and rituals are observed until its completion. To offer Kanwar is considered as the highest ritual. (see also Ch. Six).
2. *Chaturath Koti Rudra Sanhita.*

2 Sacred Specialists

Caset Identification

THE SACRED specialists of Deoghar are from three Brahmanical groups, i.e. Maithil, Radhi and Kankubj[1]. Besides, there are a few non-Brahmanic specialists, i.e. Pariyar Khatree or Pergha, Goswamis, florist, barber, *dholkiya*, *sikdar* and others. They fully or partly depend on the sacred geography of Deoghar for their livelihood. Brahmanical specialists have, however, been treated at length in this chapter.

The total population of the Pandas of Deoghar in 1971 was 11,000[2]. All the three Brahmanic Pandas come from distinct cultural groups. Profession of priestcraft has brought them on a common saddle. They are commonly known as Panda in terms of their social identification.

Maithil

Maithils constitute the bulk of the total population of the Pandas of Deoghar. In the absence of any record it is difficult to trace the origin of Maithils working as Pandas at Deoghar. However, on the basis of their Bahi[3] they can't be older than 350 years. A very few have Bahi, of more than 350 years, counting the declaration letter of their Jajman. Further, local historians[4] hold three views regarding their origin at Deoghar. According to the first opinion Maithils came in the 17th century to seek assistance from the king of Gidhaur and secured his favour on condition that they will act as Pujaris (Shrine priests) of Baidyanath temple. The second view is that the Maithils came here in search of employment. They found Baidyanath temple and ample land for agriculture. They started cultivation and worship of Baidyanath Jee. Even to this day some of the Maithils of Athganwa are cultivators and the Maithil Pandas either have kinsmen or landed property in these eight villages. But it is not unlikely that they decided to become its custodians after seeing good prospects from the temple. The third view is that once King Narendra Deo Singh of Mithila (1743-1760 A.D.) wanted to feed Brahmins to be freed from Brahmhatya (sin incurred by killing of a Brahmin) but could not get them in adequate numbers in Mithila as many of them had migrated to Deoghar.

Maithil Pandas are commonly known as Jha Jee or Baba among the pilgrims. They have different Gotras and Mulgrams which play an important role in their life. Twenty out of every hundred Maithil Pandas could not tell their Mulgram[5] which refer to their place of origin. It is their native place. They add it as title to remember the village of their origin. They can be classified in the following categories on the basis of clan and Mulgram. (Table 2.1)

Table 2.1 : Categories on the basis of Clan and Mulgram

Clan	Mulgram	Surname
1. Bharadwaj	Bilonchigeah	Ojha, Jha, Dwari, Gaiwal and Mathpals
2. Sandilya	Sadarpurye Katma, Sadarpurye Digaum, Yogwarey Bhargam, Tallanpur Arenwar	Mishra, (Sadarpurye Kalma, Sadarpurye Dijaum, Yagwarey, Tanpuray and Anrewar
3. Kashyap	Khawarey Pithanpura, Khawarey Natese, Biliyaset Narsam, Pratihost, Narantak	Khawarey, Khawarey Pithanpura Kasiya, Khawarey, Gora Khawarey, Pratihost Baliyase Narsam, Pilliwar Mishra, Panrwee Pholari, Narayan and Jha
4. Katyayan	Kunjilwar, Mandaliya	Kunjilwar, Jha, Mandaliya
5. Vatsa	Soinwar, Sarauni	Sanrewar, Jha, Soniwar and Sourauni

Maithil Pandas having common Mulgram consider each other as kith and kins. Mulgram also plays a dominant role in their marriage. Mulgram is exogamous.

Radhi

Radhi Brahmins are also functioning as Pandas of Deoghar and are commonly known as Chakratee or Bengalee Panda.

Demographically they are next to Maithil and came two generations after the Maithil settled at Deoghar. They distinguish themselves from Kankubj and Maithil on the basis of custom, title and their traditional profession of preparing chandan, daily, to offer to Baidyanath. It is interesting to note that though they are Bengalee they have more non-Bengalee Jajmans. They have their Jajmans in Pakistan and Bangladesh also who continue to send their annual Daxina. Like Maithil, Radhis are also of a different gotra Radhi Brahmins are also functioning as Pandas of Deoghar and are commonly known as Chakravarty, Bengalee or Chandanwala Panda. Demographically they are next to Maithil. According to a genealogical table, issued by the Burdwan High Court in connection with a litigation, Baninath Chakravarty and his sons were simply devotees of Baidyanath. But his grandsons took up the profession of priestcraft and Kriparam was the first to make Jajmans. Another court paper, issued in the course of a litigation over the share and right, is the Chadhawa (money and sacred articles offered to Baidyanath as well as in temple), of 1797. Bengalee Sambal corresponding to 1791 A.D. declares their traditional right of preparing Chandan for Baba and share in the Chadhawa. Since 1791 Chandanwala is their professional title.

Radhi identify themselves differently from Maithil and Kankubj on the basis of social custom, title and the traditional profession of preparing Chandan. Like Maithil, Radhi are also of different gotras, i.e. Bharadwaj, Sandilya and Kashyap.

Chatterjee is dohitra (daughter's son) of Chakravarty. One of the Chakravarty's daughter became widow in fifth generation and her sons were allowed to adopt the profession of priestcraft and since then they are Pandas of Deoghar.

Though the Chakravartys have only one professional title they identify themselves with their lineage. They consider themselves superior to Banerjees and Chatterjees because the latter are Dohitra. It is the Chakravartys alone who bring Belchandan from the nearby forest and prepare Chandan which is offered during Sringar and is distributed in the morning as Gham Chandan. To offer Chandan to pilgrims after taking Daxina is the traditional right of Chakravartys. They get a fixed amount of Arwa rice and money and five paise-in-a-rupee share in the Chadhawa daily from Sardar Panda for preparing Chandan on behalf of lord Baidyanath's estate. Each family prepares Chandan rotationally and distributes the total income of the day among the family members, if any.

Kankubj

There is a lot of controversy over the time of Kankubj's immigration. Functionally they are contemporary to each other. As Maithil became Dwari, Chakravarty became Chandanwala, similarly Kankubj became Murchchalwala. There are a few Kankubj who recently immigrated to Deoghar and tried to become Panda but were too late to get Jajmanika, so they are selling Gangajal in Lord Baidyanath's precincts. Further, a few Kankubj families are the Purohita of Maithil Panda. Kankubj Pandas are also from three gotras of a village, i.e. Kashyap, Sandilya and Bharadwaj.

Nickname associated with individual characteristics

Besides the above mentioned titles Pandas have numerous nicknames by which they are often addressed, viz. Kanphata, Lambodar, Nepali, Adhaia, Panda, etc. These nicknames are generally used for the convenience of pilgrims. Some of these are clearly indicative of individual characteristics, for instance, Kanphata (one with a split ear) or Lambodar (one with long bulging belly). Though the men for whom these terms were first used are no longer alive their sons and grandsons are affixing such nicknames to identify themselves. Similarly Nepali, Rajasthani, Oriya, etc., refer to one's Jajmanika geography.

Surname after lineage

Lineage is an important mark in the profession of priestcraft. Pandas suffix their lineage man's name to identify themselves, i.e. Shankar Panda Bhairab Panda. Here Shankar Panda identifies himself with Bhairab Panda since he comes from that lineage. Such identification is also meant for the convenience of pilgrims. Old pilgrims identify the present generation of Pandas with their lineage. While introducing themselves to pilgrims they suffix to their names the lineage title. There may be more than one Panda of the same name but two persons with one name in a lineage is impossible.

Hence, lineage as title gives the guarantee that their Jajmans cannot be taken away by another Panda.

Surname associated with residence

A few titles are associated with their respective residences. Titles like Aambari or Lohabari signify a distinctive character of residences. If first an Aam (mango), tree was planted in the house Aambari is suffixed to the title. Similarly, if first an abundance of iron was used in the house Lohabari is suffixed to the title.

Surname associated with specialisation in priestcraft

Murchchalwala is the title of the Kankubj Panda which indicates his specific duty, fanning of Lord Baidyanath with peacock feathers. Pandey of the Bharadwaj clan have the traditional right to fan Baba during Sringar. Bashawala is the common title for all Kankubj Pandas. Similarly Dwari and Chandanwala are the professional titles of Maithil and Chakravarty respectively.

Residence

The area around Baidyanath temple is inhabited by Pandas and is known as Panda-toli. Chakravartys occupy the central place of the Panda-toli which is known as Chakravarty Lane. Kankubj live in one area of the Panda-toli which is known as Pandey Lane. While inhabiting in a common place they maintain their identity by this arrangement.

In their old residence they share among themselves common living arrangements as required by their profession. The ground floor of a house is meant for Jajmans and the upper portion is meant for the Panda's personal use. The room design of the ground floor differs from the upper portion so far as sauchasthan (toilet) and windows are concerned. Just after the sauchasthan is a well which is followed by small rooms with kitchen facilities. These rooms generally don't have proper ventilation. The upper portion does not have any sauchasthan or well but each house has a window or door opening towards Baidyanath temple. It has been constructed with a view that each member has the darshan of Baidyanath as soon as he awakens in the morning.

Now, a few Pandas are residing away from Panda-toli in modern buildings due to an increase in the population and secular education and also because the original residences are in a dilapidated condition. Young Pandas don't want to live in single compact residences, hence they are shifting to different localities in which their Jajmans have donated houses. Adjoining areas have been developed into commercial centres to cater to the needs of Pandas and their Jajmans. Most of the important shops are located in these areas. Vegetable markets, recreational centres like a cinema hall, library, 'Kirtanasthan' etc., are located close to Panda-toli. Thus, like the Pandas of Gaya and Rajgir they too have their common residential territory and have single residence pattern which distinguishes the Panda of Deoghar from the secular population.

Dress

Dhoti and ganjee (vest) are the traditional dress of the Panda of Deoghar. His style of wearing dhoti is called Konchidar or Bangala. Fineness or coarseness of the dhoti a Panda wears depends on what he gets from his Jajmans. His upper part of the body is covered with a ganjee and wears a sacred thread and wears a silken chadar (long cloth) on his shoulder. He pastes bhabhut (ash of sandal burnt at Baidyanath Sacred centre) on his forehead. A long tik (tuft of hair on head) adorns him. One may be modern in his dress but he cannot cut his tik without being subjected to social criticism.

Pandas wear Pitambari (yellow silken cloth) in their ceremonial dress. They wear it while performing sacred performances at the Baidyanath Cluster during Basant Panchami, Shivaratri, or whenever they go to attend any social function.

They do not wear shoes or slippers throughout the day but the use of kharaun (wooden slippers) is popular. They wear shoes or chappals only during a Jajmanika tour.

Dialect

Panda's dialect is different from average Deoghariya dialect. Though they come from three different dialectic groups they have a similar professional dialect. Another point which attracts our attention is that a Chakravarty speaks Khari Hindi and Punjabi fluently with his Jajmans from Delhi and Punjab respectively. Similarly others also speak the dialect of their respective Jajmanika geography. Panda dialect has been shaped under the influence of Maithali, Santhali, Magahi and Hindi. There are numerous examples to supplicate this statement. Majority of the Panda are from Mithila. Deoghar is in the district of Santhal Parganas having Santhali population. Further, it was under the rule of Nawab of Bengal and a section of the Pandas hails from Bengal. Again the adjoining areas are inhabited by the Magahi-speaking people and for sometime it was within the Kingdom of Magadh. Further it was also a pocket of Swadeshi movement which established a Hindi school called Gobardhan Hindi Vidyapeeth. Most of the Pandas receive their early education in Sanskrit at this Vidyapeeth. All this have contributed to the development of a dialect known as Panda dialect.

Food habits

Pandas of Deoghar with certain exceptions among Kankubj have similar food habits but they differ from the Pandas of Basukinath and other places because they are non-vegetarian. They are fond of delicious dishes. And this is one of the topics of discussion after return from a Jajmanika tour. Sardar Panda has a special cook in his kitchen to prepare delicious non-vegetarian dishes.

Their traditional food gives them a distinctive place among the people of Deoghar. They take fried chura or sweets in Jalkhaie and rice, pulse (very little) varieties of green (more in quantity), ghee and either milk or curd at lunch and chura dahi (curd) and sweets at supper. Families which cooked in the evening were regarded as poor and were subjected to social criticism. Though food habits have changed to a great extent the cultural values of food are still the same.

Now, owing to pressing pecuniary conditions Pandas generally take breakfast in shops (hotel, restaurant) according to their convenience. At lunch quality and quantity have been curtailed whereas at supper bread, greens and milk are consumed. Meat and fish are important dishes of the community. Chakravarty and Maithil are traditionally non-vegetarian while Kankubj learnt it from their neighbours. They don't use onion or garlic while preparing meat and fish for a social dinner but individually they consume it. Generally, ghee is used more than onion and garlic. "Pawa seer ghee" (250 grams) in "Ek seer mansa" (1kg. meat) is a popular saying among them. According to a myth, once the bawarchi (cook) of a Nawab was not pleased with his master. So he left his master's place and decided to return home. To salute the king of the region was the custom of that time. So while crossing this place he saluted the then Sardar Panda and narrated his grief. Sardar Panda ordered him to cook meat. He was also told that onion and garlic must not be used since he was a Brahmin. So he used 250 grams (pawa) of ghee in one seer meat. Thus from that day it became popular in the community.

Bari is another delicious and important dish of the community. Paron is also an important dish of the community which is made of milk, barley, *chchohara* (beaten rice), kismis, giri (copra), ilaichi (cardamom) and sugar. Similarly is Tikhur, an important preparation of the community made with Tikhur milk, sugar and some spices. *Sabudana* (sago) is the most important dish prepared during marriage. There is keen competition in preparing sabudana and meat during marriage. Unlike Gaiwal there is no rule about who would serve first among the family members. Usually a woman does not eat before her husband has finished but she may eat in case the husband is out of station or is returning home late. Anyone can prepare food. Generally young daughters or daughters-in-law prepare and distribute food. They are allowed to prepare even during menstruation. They first offer cooked food to the fire god and cow. This is locally known as "Bhoga Lagana."

They don't eat kacchi (rice, pulse, etc.) with their Jajman, but can take pucci (fried bread, etc.). They consume kacchi only when that has been prepared by their own caste men (subcaste) or by himself. There was no interdining among the Pandas of the three groups but now due to spread of education, etc. such restrictions are vanishing. However, even today, there are many orthodox Pandas who don't eat or even drink water outside their homes.

Pastimes and hobbies

A Panda is generally in the habit of chewing flaked betel nut. Even while assisting Jajman in the temple Pandas chew the nut. Not only males but famales also invariably chew betel. The latter develop this habit after marriage. If one is not habituated of betel he takes snuff or khaini.

Bhaang is an important intoxicant. It is taken in a group and go for Nibatney (toilet). There are numerous small groups and are known as Bhaang Butti Samaj. Members of each such Samaj belong to a particular age group. Usually a Bhaang Butti Samaj has members only from its own community, for example, a Bhaang Bhutti Samaj of Chakravartys necessarily has membership only from Chakravartys. The sole function of such a Samaj is to prepare Bhaang for its members while doing Nibatney at 2.30 p.m.; at this moment they cover the distance of 3 to 6 miles and return in the evening before Sringar. At this moment small groups in action are worth watching.

Wrestling is another hobby. There are four gymnasia in the community to train the youth. Nowadays it is gradually losing its importance because it is not considered good. Education is given more importance now.

Bird-fight is another important hobby of the Pandas. They are fond of having a variety of birds. Sardar Panda has a miniature zoo. "Bulbul's" flight is a matter of competition and it is one of the hobbies. Sometimes one spends thousands of rupees on procuring a suitable "Bulbul" as a match. There was a Bachwa Bulbul of Lohabari which continuously won competitions and remained Deoghar Champion for seven years. Now the Bulbul of a Khawarey is Deoghar Champion for the last three years. These matches are very interesting and worth watching and are usually organised in winters and continue till the following day of Makarsankranti. Competitions are organized on Tuesdays and Fridays. If a Bulbul is of a high standard, it is used only once in a week for match purposes. It gets no food for twentyfour hours before the match. Championship matches are held at Tapovan on the Makarsankranti day. Champion Bulbul is taken out in a big procession on a silver throne to Baidyanath Sacred Centre and it remains the Champion till Durga Puja. A goat is offered to Parvatee Jee and a Bhandara is organised for the comrades by the owner of the Champion Bulbul.

Music is also an important hobby of the Pandas. One of them said, "we are interested in music and it is one of our hobbies. But it is gradually decreasing. There are two musical organisations in the community. But it is true that these days the young are more interested in movie music than in classical music. There were many famous musicians in our community who were invited from Calcutta and other places for musical performances. Nowadays we have one such musical organization whose members are invited from different corners of the country. Most of us know Jhumar and Bhajans of Vidyapati which we sing frequently. You will find a number of poets in our community".

REFERENCES

1. Kankubjs are originally the Brahmins of Kanoj hence Kankubj.
2. As enumerated by the Special officer, Deoghar Municipality, on the basis of municipal records, vide his letter No. 209 dated 19.2.1971.
3. The book recording the names of pilgrims visiting the shrine of Baidyanath. Each Panda records the names of those pilgrims who were associated with him as his clients or Jajmans. The Jajmani relationship between the Panda and the Pilgrim is maintained hereditarily on the basis of the Bahi which might be called a reference book of Jajman relationship.
4. Mishra, Badrinarain, *Maithils of Deoghar*, 1964.

Sacred Specialists
Life-Cycle

3

BIRTH, CHILDHOOD AND SOCIALIZATION

PANDAS of Deoghar believe that a child is the gift of Lord Baidyanath. Barren women are considered as a social disgrace of the community. Non-attainment of parenthood is considered as the wrath of Baidyanath. Delay in conception leads to performance of numerous rituals. As it appears from various case histories vows are taken in the name of Baidyanath to be blessed with a child.

Several rituals are observed on the first sign of pregnancy. Delicious dishes come from the woman's Naiher (mother's house) regularly from conception to Chchathi (ceremony of the sixth day of the birth). Expecting woman worship Kuldeota (lineage deity) Baidyanath and Sitla in the sixth month. The same set of gods and goddess are worshipped in the ninth month. They get Baba's Prasad (sacred ingredients offered to Baidyanath), i.e. Gham Chandan (Sandal) from the sixth month until delivery, and the child would be faithful to Baidyanath and remain a faithful Panda of Deoghar. For easy and safe delivery, a woman is given paan (betel) and mahua's flowers (an intoxicant flower) as prasad of Kuldeota (lineage deity) in the ninth month. Social taboos imposed on a pregnant Pandaine (female Panda) are similar to other communities of north India.

A Dagrin (female sweeper) is called for safe birth. A male child is preferred to a female. Oldest women of the family worship Kuldeota (lineage deity) Baidyanath and Sitla just after a birth. First of all Charnamrit (of water made holy after offering) of Baidyanath is given to newly born baby until the sixth day for longevity and sound health. Among the

Maithil delicious dishes come from the naiher (parental house) of the new mother. There is no such custom among the Chakravartys and Kankubj. Since women's parental houses are always far off from Deoghar, Naehar (local) and other devotional songs dedicated to Baidyanath are sung by women from the first to the sixth day till Chchathi, the ceremony performed on the sixth day of the birth, is performed. The Chchathi of a male child or of the first issue is performed with great pomp and show. Vows taken in the name of Baidyanath are executed on this day. A community dinner is served to lineage men. Before serving the dinner, Baidyanath as well as Kuldeota and Sitla are worshipped with Sodsoupchar (sixteen ingredients). A goat is offered to goddess Parvatee and then served in the community dinner. Among Maithil, Fua and Fufa (father's sister and her husband) are invited to worship Lord Baidyanath and to prepare *Kajal* (black soot for the eyes) for which they get clothes, ornaments, rice, etc., as Neg (customary). But among Chakravartys and Kankubjs these rituals are executed by the oldest women of the family.

At the time of weaving food is offered to Baidyanath. Initiation ceremony is performed at the fifth year of a male child when a man well-versed in sacred texts initiates the child and first of all the name of Lord Baidyanath is written. From this day onward the boy is trained for Pandagiri. After a year or so he goes under rigorous training to learn Sandhya Mantra, Baidyanath Mahatam, Shiv Puran, etc. Then he works with his father or the head of the family and learns how to assist and guide Jajmans. He does not attend any regular class or read any book but simply sits on the traditional Gaddi and observes the activities of elders. Thus by observation he learns how to assist a Jajman and also learns the different languages of different Jajmans, is familiarized with Jajmans and Jajmanika. He also learns to maintain Jajmanika bahi (client register). This is how primary professional socialization of a Panda takes place. One attends school only after this kind of socialization. Formal schooling and profession go side by side.

Upnayan

Upnayan (sacred thread ceremony) is essential for Brahmins. It is enjoined on them by the scriptures. It has been said that all men are Sudras by birth and this sacred-thread ceremony gives the status of the "twice-born" which include Brahmins, Kshatris and Vaishyas. Its importance is acknowledged more by Brahmins than the other two Varnas.

Age for performing Upnayan is governed by Garbhastak (eight years from the date of conception) rule among the Pandas of Deoghar which prescribes that an Upnayan must be performed within or up to eight years and this period is counted from conception. Guru (teacher) initiates one with certain mantras which one is expected to follow. One gets detailed training in Sanskritic texts after Upnayan. One becomes entitled to assist pilgrims in performing Sankalpa (final ritual) only after Upnayan. One learns the art of priesthood and how to maintain personal purity from elderly family members. One now keeps "Sikha" or "Tik" (tuft of hair at the back of the head) and maintains it in the later part of life. One becomes a member of the Bhaang Butti Samaj. Depending on one's interest one also gets training in wrestling, music, etc.

Adolescence and marriage

Children obey their parents, who are considered next to Baidyanath. They remain under the control of their parents even after attaining adolescence. A boy or a girl has no voice in selecting a life partner. A boy respects the elder brother and receives affection in return. They discuss important matters among themselves. They always try to have a mutual understanding and fairly share Jajmanika. Husband is considered as God. Being Ardhangani (the best half) a wife shares the joys and sorrows of her husband and also claims share in the Papa (evil deeds) or Punya (merit) of her husband. She never takes the name of her husband.

Marriage is an important event among the Pandas. Maithils practise early marriage with certain exceptions. They practise local endogamy like the Pandas of Gaya and Rajgir. In selecting a life-partner they follow clan and Mul exogamy. Their population is so large that they hardly have any problem in settling a marriage. Marriage gives full ritual status to a Panda of Deoghar and enables him to participate in all the rituals and social activities. Generally they practise monogamy but there are instances of polygamy also. The marriage customs of Maithils are unique in the sense that women play an important and exclusive role in the negotiations. They generally visit one another's house and in the course of these visits they select a boy for their daughter and grand-daughter. They first express their desire before the female members of the boy and if the latter agrees then the girl's side sends the head of the family to negotiate with the boy's side. Sindur Pinha-Pinhi is observed after negotiations are finalised and the male members execute Hanth Banh Dastkhat at the Baidyanath Sacred Centre and the *Dharm Raxhni Society registers it. Lagna (date, time, etc. of marriage) is fixed at this moment. The Barat (marriage procession) leaves for the bride's place just after the custom of Darwaja Lagana to resume their professional activities. No male member remains present except the bride's father. All rituals are performed in the presence of the female members of both sides and on this day only the female members of the groom's party are served dinner and the male members enjoy the dinner in the evening of the following day. Most of the Pandas join a Barat Party at Baidyanath temple when it comes to worship Baidyanath.

The bride returns from her husband's house after a week and remains in her father's house at least for a year. To deliver the first issue in Naihar (mother's house) is the custom of the community. Exchange of gifts is maintained with great zeal from marriage day until Dwriragaman.

Unlike Maithils, Chakravartys and Kankubjs practise late marriage. Also Kankubj and Chakravarty women have no say in a marriage. It is negotiated and settled by male members outside Deoghar. Chakravartys generally settle their marriages in West Bengal and Kankubjs in U.P. The marriage of a daughter is generally fixed outside the Panda community and a Bahu (daughter-in-law) is also brought from a non-Panda community. This leads to problems of adjustment. A woman either coming from different community or going to a

*Dharm Raxhni Society is the Social Organization of Pandas of Deoghar.

different community feels numerous difficulties in a new environment. She finds herself unable to adjust within the new community and this results in a broken family. There are numerous examples of daughters returning home on account of maladjustment in a new family. Wives of several young Pandas have deserted their husbands on this account.

Daily routine

The daily routine of life that a Maithil Panda leads is not very different from that of a Chakravarty or a Kankubj. The Panda wakes up early in the morning before "Sarkari Puja" which is performed between 3.30 and 4.30 a.m. (the time varies from season to season). He meditates on Lord Baidyanath and other deities on the premises, chants slokas and then leaves his bed. Free from the daily duty he participates in the Sarkari Puja. He offers Kachajal to Lord Baidyanath and other deities of this premises. Taking Jalkhaie he sits on his Gaddi to assist and guide Jajmans till the temple is closed. During the day while he is in the temple he enquires about the arrival of Jajmans, and also goes home to take his meals followed by rest for an hour or so. Then he returns to the temple and sits on his Gaddi or on the way at any shop to inquire about the arrival of Jajmans. Then he goes for Nibetney (toilet), and then to the Bhaang Butti Samaj and takes Bhaang. He either takes bath or changes clothes after returning from Nibetney and goes to the Math with the Jajman, if any, to guide and assist him. He remains here till all his Jajmans have finished the sacred performances. He inquires about the arrival of Jajmans, if any, from time to time. Finally he returns home. He takes his meals and discusses the domestic issues while eating. Then he retires but before this he once again remembers Lord Baidyanath and all other deities of the temple premises.

Death and the rituals

The Pandas of Deoghar believe that they remain with Baidyanath Jee owing to their pious service. Numerous rituals are associated with the death of a Panda which distinguish them from the secular population of Deoghar. As soon as the death occurs Bhumisajja (laying on floor) is given to the deceased

Panda. A Rudraxa mala offered to Baidyanath Jee is put round his neck in the belief that it will help him reach Lord Baidyanath. Bhasma is also pasted on his forehead as Lord Baidyanath's Prasad. Bhaang, Dhatura and Belpatra are kept near the head of the deceased in the same belief. The deceased is also given Charnamrit of Lord Baidyanath as well as a new Dhoti and Chadar. All these are not only considered as Prasad but it is also believed that these will enable the deceased in reaching near Lord Baidyanath where he may have the opportunity to serve him again.

Ekadasha is performed on the eleventh day of the death in which a social dinner is given to Bhaiyaro (lineage men). Meat is essentially served on this occasion. Maithils invite Chakravartys and Kankubjs on the twelfth day. Similarly Chakravartys and Kankubjs invite Maithils on the twelfth day but Chakravartys and Kankubjs invite one another on the eleventh day. Ekodist is an important ritual which is performed annually by the Pandas of Deoghar.

Death at matured old age is considered as summons from the Baba to be one of his courtiers, but premature death is believed to be the wrath of the Baba and the dead become ghosts.

Social Interactions on Intra- and Inter-Group Levels 4

PANDAS of Deoghar are organized Bhaiyaro or Gotiyaro which indicates lineage or Vansa. The number of the families has considerably increased since they first came to Deoghar. For instance, Aambari and Lohabari, the two original families of Maithil Pandas of Deoghar, have now grown into fortyeight and thirty families respectively. All families belonging to a lineage do not always form a happy kin group. More often than not they fall into professional rivalries. But on social and ceremonial occasions like marriage, birth, death they come together and express their kinship ties by exchange of gifts. All Pandas are related to one another within their caste groups which they recognize as *Munch Dadhi ka Sambandh* a kind of kinship bond which obliges male members to shave off hair and moustaches in case of a death occurring within that kin group. Exchange of gifts and visits are associated with prestige. Those who do not follow this rule of kinship are subjected to social criticism.

Priestcraft has broken the bond of territorial and sub-caste differences. Pandas of three caste groups i.e. Maithil, Kankubj and Chakravarty, consider themselves as one and, emotionally, as relatives. There are several instances of Pandas uniting against non-Pandas in disputes between the two. On such occasions the Pandas ignore their personal differences, professional rivalries or sub-caste distinctions. However, within the community relationship between the members of different sub-castes is not always very close.

Maithils outnumber and claim to be older than Kankubjs and Chakravartys. They consider Chakravartys and Kankubjs inferior to them. Traditionally Maithils neither invite Chakravartys and Kankubjs for ceremonial dinners on the day they invite their castemen nor dine with them. But after independence they all interdine. The three upjatis of Pandas visit each other during marriages and other ceremonial occasions. Female members of the three upjatis hardly visit members of other than their own upjatis.

Professionally, Pandas form a homogeneous community but they do maintain their identity in their customs, residence, style of life and different rights over Baidyanath temple. The members of each upjati have limited social inter-course with the members of the other than their own upjatis. There are representatives from each upjati in the Dharmraxhni society according to their population. Except Maithils others don't have the right to become the Sardar Panda of Baidyanath. Like Maithils, Chakravartys also claim to be older and professionally superior to Kankubjs at Deoghar. Earlier, Kankubjs had limited social relationship with Maithils and Chakravartys. Neither Kankubjs were invited by Maithils and Chakravartys nor were the Kankubjs invited by them but are now inviting Maithils and Chakravartys and are also being invited by them. Socially the Pandas of Deoghar interact on the basis of their caste identification.

Panda-Jajman relationship

The very term Panda indicates the individual or the community having a good number of Jajmans. The three upjatis of Pandas, i.e. Maithil, Chakravarty and Kankubjs, have Jajmans. Since Maithils are more in number their Jajmanika geography is vast.

Maithils, Kankubjs, and Chakravartys are first, second and third in the matter of the total number of Jajmans and Jajmanika geography. They have their Jajmans in Nepal, Bangladesh, Pakistan and in other countries of Asia where Hinduism is practised. Jajmans who are unable to come here annually send their Daxina. It reflects their contribution in uniting and bringing Jajmans of different nations on a common platform. Profession of priestcraft has given these three upjatis' Pandas a ground on which they enter into a traditional relationship with their Jajmans. Pandas have a twofold relationship with their Jajmans. First, when a Panda visits his Jajmans and, second, when Jajmans undertake pilgrimage to Baidyanathdham. This relationship has been practised since time immemorial and it is traditionally transferred from one generation to another, by both. The Panda-

Jajman relationship will be broadly discussed under two categories, i.e. Panda undertaking Jajmanika tour and Jajmans undertaking pilgrimage to Deoghar. First we will discuss Panda pilgrim interactions at Deoghar.

As prescribed by Hinduism, Hindus undertake pilgrimage to Baidyanathdham with different purposes but generally they come for a happy and prosperous life and to earn merit for the next life. It is not difficult for a pilgrim to find out his traditional Panda even if he is not familiar with him. Usually Pandas recognise their Jajmans from their native place, caste and lineage and convince their Jajmans of their genuineness by showing the Bahi (register) in which Jajmans ancestors' names and signatures are preserved. Jajmans pay respect to their Pandajee and consider him as the servant of Baidyanath and also as next to Baidyanath. A Panda is considered as the middleman between the pilgrim and Baidyanath. A pilgrim is received either by the Panda himself or by his Gumasta (servant) at Baidyanathdham, if necessary, with the Bahi (register). The Panda enquires after a Jajman's welfare. If the Jajman wants to stay there then he takes him to his lodge and provides him with all the amenities. He takes the Jajman to Baidyanathjee and assists and guides him in performing the rituals at different sacred centres and lastly the Jajman performs Sankalpa. Conventionally they enquire after the welfare of the Jajman twice a day, i.e. before leaving for the temple in the morning and before Sringar (decoration in evening of Baidyanath) in the evening. A Jajman is further assisted and guided during Sringar. If a Jajman stays for more than a day then the same routine is followed otherwise the Jajman is given a warm send-off. The Jajman is given Bibhuti (sacred powder) and Charnamrit (holy water) for his family members at the time of his departure. The Panda takes the Jajman's signature in the Dastkhati bahi (signature register) with date. Thus, whenever a Jajman comes the abovementioned interactions occur and these activities contribute towards strengthening the Jajman-Panda relationship. Beside, in some cases, Jajmans maintain regular correspondence with their Panda. In case a Jajman does not visit Baidyanathdham, he requests his Panda to be excused and sends his annual daxina, similarly the Panda also reminds his Jajman for his annual daxina through letters. The P&T

department also serves as an agent in strengthening the Jajman-Panda relationship. One special postal peon has been deputed by the authorities to deliver letters and money orders to the Pandas in Baidyanath temple.

Panda on tour

A Panda undertakes Jajmanika tour with a double purpose, i.e. to realize annual daxina and dues, if any, and to regulate the traditional Panda-Jajman relationship and, if possible, to make new Jajmans through new contacts.

On the basis of such Jajmanika tours Pandas can be classified into two categories:

(i) Those who undertake a Jajmanika tour once in a year. To this category of Panda's Jajmans belong men from business or service class.
(ii) Those who undertake a Jajmanika tour twice in a year. The Jajmans in this case are mostly farmers.

Pandas undertake Jajmanika tours generally in a slack season (when the influx of pilgrims is low) or during the harvest season. They always consider the convenience of Jajmans while undertaking a Jajmanika tour. There is no hard and fast rule in the community regarding Jajmanika tours a Panda can undertake. The number of such visits increases or decreases according to one's necessity, ceremonial occasions and mode of relationship with Jajmans. If there is a marriage in a Jajman's family the Panda may attend it in the capacity of Tirth Guru, and in the case of a marriage in his own family the Panda may go to seek financial assistance from his Jajmans. The Panda usually seeks Jajmans' assistance in distress and adverse circumstances also.

A Panda consults an astrologer before undertaking a Jajmanika tour to avoid ominous period or if he himself is well versed in this subject he may personally fix an auspicious period. An officiating person is selected and entrusted to look after the profession of priestcraft in his absence. In case of there being only a minor male member in the family then Gotiya Bhai are entrusted to assist the minor member as also to assist and guide pilgrims in the performance of Sankalpa.

He stores pera (a kind of sweetmeat) ilaichidana (cardamom seed), sindur (vermillion) and Bibhuti (sacred powder) to distribute among the Jajmans. He salutes Baidyanath before leaving for the journey and for his safe return and welfare.

As soon as the bus or train he travels in moves he chants a few shlokas. He does not eat anything in any hotel or eating house. If the journey is long he may be carrying his food. Those who can afford take a Gumasta (servant) with them. Usually a servant carries his belongings and a Gumasta assists him in collecting Daxina and in performing regular rituals. It is interesting to note that a Panda who is irregular in performing his daily rituals at Deoghar performs them regularly when on a tour just to impress his Jajmans. He gives the incidental expenses to the Gumasta. A Gumasta also gets bidaie (customary gift at the time of departure) from the Jajmans.

Life during a Jajmanika tour is different from the one a Panda leads at Deoghar. He may remain on a tour for a month or more. He stays with his Jajmans. He awakes in the morning remembering Lord Baidyanath and other deities of Baidyanathjee cluster and his Guru in the morning and performs Karnika, Gayetri and other Japs and applies sandal on his forehead after taking a bath. Taking Jalkhaie he moves from one Jajman to another to collect dues and annual daxina. In the villages, his daxina is generally kept in a shop, fixed by him, from where he collects money is exchange of the grain daxina. He takes his midday meal with any Jajman and rests there. His lunch consists of Puris (prepared by Jajman) or prepares rice himself or his Gumasta prepares rice, pulses, greens etc. for him. He drinks Bhaang (an intoxicant) in the afternoon and goes for Nibetney (toilet). Once again he moves from one Jajman to another. He performs Sandhya, Karnika Jap, etc., in the evening also. Like in the morning he stays with any Jajman in the night also and broadly, similar routine is followed all through his tour days.

As a Panda approaches the house of a Jajman he starts blessing him and his family members on behalf of Lord Baidyanath and inquires about there welfare. He pastes Bibhuti on their foreheads and distributes Sindur (vermillion), among female Jajmans. He then asks for a plate in which he offers Prasad of the Baba. At the time of his leaving, in addition to the dues and annual daxina he also gets bidaie (customary gift at the time of departure) from each Jajman. In this way he visits his Jajmans, realizes his annual dues daxina with the promise of a visit the following year. The same cycle is again followed, the main purpose behind such visits being to keep alive the traditional Panda-Jajman relationship.

Immediately after his return from a Jajmanika tour a Panda leaves for the Baidyanath temple to salute the Baba and, on return, he performs Gayetri or Sandhya and other Japs. He narrates his experiences to his family members, meets the kinsmen to whom he had assigned the job of assisting and guiding Jajmans and exchanges experiences with them and the relatives. Then he retires. Routine life at Deoghar starts from next morning.

Panda-Guru relationship

Guru is he who gives training in sacred activities and teaches sacred texts. He commands high respect in the community. Pandas seek his guidance at the time of entering the profession of a priest, i.e. at the time of Upnayan. Gurus play an important role in their life. They can be classified into three categories: (i) Initiating Guru, (ii) Kul Guru, and (iii) Purificatory Guru.

Initiating guru

While performing Upnayan a Guru is needed to initiate in the Sandhya Mantra, etc. He teaches the process and method of executing the sacred performances. Generally the eldest or most educated member of the family acts as Guru at such times. For example, Dada (grandfather), Chacha (uncle), Fufa (father's sister's husband), Nana (maternal grandfather), or Mamu (maternal uncle) act as the initiating Guru.

Kul guru

Kul Guru is the guru of the whole lineage. It is desirable that whole lineage be his disciple but it is optional for the lineage members. He is also worshipped at the time of worshipping the Kuldeota.

Purificatory guru

He is the Guru who finally initiates a Panda to achieve the truth of life. He is needed after the stage of grihastashram (family life). This guru commands high respect in the community and is annually worshipped by the disciples. He also receives annual daxina from his disciples. A Purificatory Guru is also optional.

Panda-Purohit relationship

Hindus need assistance of a Brahmin in performing any ritual. Pandas of Deoghar are firstly Hindu and then Panda. Being Hindu they naturally seek the assistance of a Brahmin in performing any ritual. There are a few Maithils and Kankubjs, not from Panda family, who assist and guide Pandas in the performance of rituals. A Panda consults a Purohit at the time of a Jajmanika tour, Upnayan, marriage, death, etc., and Satyanarain Katha on any festive day. There is nothing like annual or monthly daxina for the Purohit. They are paid at the end of a ritual. Though both are Brahmin Purohit never eats with his Jajman. By having Purohit, Pandas enter the double Jajman relationship, that is, having Jajmans and also being Jajmans of their Purohit. These families have specialised themselves in Purohiti (guiding Jajmans is performing various rituals) and it is their primary source of livelihood.

Panda-Gumasta relationship

Most of the Pandas appoint Gumastas for professional assistance. Gumasta is he who works as a general assistant of a Panda. He assists him in the profession of priestcraft as also in the domestic affairs particularly in marketing. Pandas have two kinds of relationship with their Gumastas, i.e., (i) Master-servant relationship; and (ii) Partner relationship.

A Gumasta is employed on monthly or annual wages to assist a Panda in helping and guiding Jajmans. He addresses the Panda as Malik. He also gets money from his Malik's Jajmans for his services. Relationship of a partner with a Gumasta is a recent development due to the present not-so-good economic conditions of the Pandas who are unable to maintain a paid Gumasta. The Gumasta takes half of the total daxina from a Panda for assisting him in helping and guiding a Jajman.

Nowadays a Panda generally appoints a Gumasta on salary only during the busy season. Chakravartys have appointed a

Gumasta on behalf of the whole community to prepare Chandan for the Baba (Baidyanath) which is offered during the Sarkari Puja (first ritual of the morning) and Sringar (decoration of the lingam in the evening). Permanent Gumastas are treated as family members.

Panda-Pawania relationship

Those who get Pawana (ceremonial gift) for their valuable services to Pandas rendered during different ceremonies are called Pawaniyas. They get their Pawana (customary payment and remuneration) either in cash or in kind. Ceremonies like Chchathi, Upnayan, marriage, etc., cannot be performed without their services. Pandas have a certain relationship with the Pawaniyas. Pawaniyas come from different castes and render their caste services. Following are the Pawaniyas of the Pandas of Deoghar.

Hajam (*barber*)

A barber is required during Upnayan and marriage to shave off hairs and to assist the Purohit respectively. There is no fixed amount to be paid at such occasions. Pandas have, traditionally a Naie (barber) but they do not give him anything annually. He gets his remuneration just after his ceremonial or ritual role. He is also required during Shradh (one of the death rites) to shave off hairs on the bank of the Shivganga. A Panda also needs a barber while assisting a Jajman in different rituals, i.e. Mundan, marriage, etc.

Dhobi (*washerman*)

Washerman also serves as a Pawania. He gets his remuneration just after his specific functions and no annual gift. A dhobin (washerwoman) is required during Upnayan. The boy who is to be initiated sees the face of a dhobin before his initiation. He also sits in her lap and she dances and sings carrying him. He then goes to worship Baidyanath.

Dome (*sweeper*)

Dome is popularly known as Harijan and is the lowest untouchable caste but even then he is one of the Pawaniya of the Pandas. They supply bamboo pots during Shradh (one of the death ritual). A female dome is popularly known as Dagrin and is an efficient mid-wife. Though the entry of Domin to the houses is taboo, she is welcome for the safe birth of a child. She also gets her remuneration just after completion of her role in a specific ritual or Karm (work).

Kumhar (potter)

Potters are another Pawaniya of the Pandas. They are required during Upnayan and marriage. Their visits are comparatively more frequent than of other Pawaniyas since a Panda needs earthen potteries for Jajmans also. Like other Pawaniyas potters are also paid just after the completion of a specific work.

Barhai (carpenter)

Barhai is also a Pawania and his services are required only during Upnayan. He supplies Kharaun (wooden slippers) but now most of the Pandas purchase them from the market and are being forgotten as Pawaniyas and are paid like other Pawaniyas.

Sacred Specialists
Non-Brahmin and Other Functionaries 5

Specialists connected with Ashrams

ASHRAMS (abodes of ascetics) have been briefly discussed in the sacred geography of Deoghar. Four important Ashrams of all-India importance are Balanand Brahmachari, Deo Sangh, Satsang and Paglababa Ashram. These ashrams attract converted Hindu devotees from foreign countries like Britain, America, Canada, Germany, France, etc. Besides Shivlingam representing Baidyanath, different gods and goddesses are installed in these Ashrams. The first Ashram, i.e. Balanand Brahmachari Ashram, was established in 1906 by a saint Balanand who found it a good place for penance. He was a great devotee of Baidyanath and worshipped him regularly. This ashram has the highest number of devotees. Satsang, the other important Ashram was established by Sri Thakur Anukul Chandra on 2 September, 1946. He established the ashram here owing to Baidyanath Kshetra and was worshipping Baidyanath on festive occasions. Sriniwas Angan commonly known as Paglababa Ashram was established by Sri Lilanand Thakur on 19 February, 1967, as Kshetra of Baidyanath. Baidyanath is represented here by a silver Shivalingam. Krishna is the principal deity of the ashram. Deo Sangh, locally known as Navadurga Mandir, is another ashram established by Swami Narendra Brahmachari in September, 1955. Though the principal deity of the Ashram is Bagla Devi it also represents Baidyanath through a marble Shivlingam.

Disciples of these ashrams are of two kinds, i.e. (i) those who live on the ashram campus, and (ii) those who come from outside. Disciples of the first category observe only annual sacred performances at the Baidyanath Sacred Centre while the disciples of the second category worship Baidyanath whenever they visit Deoghar.

Most of these ashrams generally don't believe in caste and creed. A disciple of these ashrams assists and guides a pilgrim at different sacred centres of the ashram. Disciples of the first category may also recite the Shiv Puran, the Ramayana etc., on the request of fellow ashramites of first category or on the request of pilgrims. Ramlila and Krishnalila are also organised by these ascetic disciples on different occasions. Founders of these ashrams are called Gurus by the disciples. The Gurus impart training to their disciples in the observing of regular sacred performances. Functionally, disciples of these ashrams and Pandas are similar in the sense that the Pandas are trained by their fathers and grand-fathers whereas these ascetic ashramites are trained by their respective Gurus in the profession of priestcraft.

The Gurus of these Ashrams are of different castes. They want to develop and spread their ashrams and to make the maximum number of disciples and devotees.

Pariyar Khatrees or Perghas

There are thirty families of Pariyar Khatrees working as Pandas of Baidyanath. They claim to be the descendants of the legendary Basuki, who has been identified as "Bhil in the Shiv Puran". They are the oldest Pandas of Basukinath. Till 1950 Baneshwar Panda of the Pariyar Khatree group was the Sardar Panda of Basukinath, and the temple was in their custody. It is said that these Pandas appointed Maithil Brahmins to worship lord Basukinath and to assist pilgrims but in course of time they lost their right over the temple and are now professionally similar to Maithils and Goswami Pandas of Basukinath.

Though under the influence of Maithil a few Pariyar Khatrees are performing Jagopawit (sacred-thread ceremony) it was not known to them. Even today some Perghas don't wear the sacred thread, and those who wear don't understand its importance. They don't know any sacred mantra. Most of them are illiterate and don't have the right to perform Sankalpa (the final ritual). This is why, conventionally, they appoint Maithil Brahmins as Gumasta (servant).

Pariyar Pandas have matrimonial relationship with the

Pariyars of Basukinath who are farmers by occupation. Their marriage customs are different from those of their professional colleagues. They don't give any social dinner before marriage but invite their kith and kin after a marriage is solemnized. Widow marriage is prevalent among them.

They don't have any professional title like the Pandas of Deoghar and Maithil Pandas of Basukinath. They wear dhoti like other Pandas. They lack professional training unlike Pandas of Deoghar or Maithil Pandas of Basukinath and have no knowledge of the sacred texts and mantras. They have appointed Maithil Brahmins to assist and guide their Jajmans in performing different rituals. They have enough agricultural land to support their families. They produce only rice with the help of Santhal servants. They are non-vegetarian and rice is their main food. Pergha's women also come to the Basukinath cluster to assist and guide pilgrims. They don't have any right to take offered money but it is in practice.

Goswami

There are two families of Goswami, belonging to the Kashyap clan, who are working as Pandas of Basukinath. Like Perghas, Goswamis also lack knowledge of the sacred texts and mantras. They resemble Perghas in their food habits, dress and customs. They establish matrimonial relationships with the Goswamis of the nearby villages who are farmers. Their Purohit gives them the sacred thread which they wear after offerings to Basukinath but are not aware of its importance. They wear it because their colleagues are wearing. They don't have any Gumasta.

There are three adults in the two families of which one is a Government servant, who has never practised his hereditary profession, one is in the profession of Pandagiri but is not in the mood to continue it if his son (the third adult member) gets a job, after doing his graduation.

Florists

We now discuss here florists, because anyone who is directly or indirectly associated with the temple will be a subject of our discussion of Deoghar and Basukinath who traditionally depend on Baidyanath and Basukinath temple.

Florist here is one who supplies flowers, garlands and other sacred articles to the pilgrims, devotees and to temple management. He may be a Mali (Florist) by Jati or he may not be. Generally to sell flowers, garlands, Belpatra, etc., is the traditional right of the Mali Jati. One of the Malis supplies flowers, garlands, Belpatra, etc., to the Baidyanath temple management. He receives an annual pawana (payment) from the Sardar Panda on behalf of Baidyanath. In addition to this Pawana he is provided with a rent-free stall at the Parvatee Sacred Centre of the Baidyanath Cluster. There are numerous other florists who sell flowers, garlands, belpatra, etc., within Baidyanath's premises but are essentially non-Pawaniyas to Baidyanath. They, traditionally, supply sacred articles to pilgrims and devotees and totally depend on this hereditary profession. They have also specialized themselves in this profession. Not only the Mali but Dhanuk, Jaiswar Kurmi and Maithil Brahmans (other than Pandas) are also functioning as florists at Deoghar and Basukinath. The Maithil Brahmins who sell sacred articles during Sringar at the Baidyanath Cluster are relatives of the late Sardar Panda. The florists irrespective of caste who have a stall at the Baidyanath cluster pay 0.50 paise daily to the Sardar Panda towards rent and conventionally this rent is deposited with the wife (in case of wives it goes to the eldest wife) of the Sardar Panda and this amount is treated as her Stridhan.

Jaiswar Kurmis, who prefer to call themselves Jaiswal the Rout, are the Pawaniyas of Basukinath since they supply flowers, belpatra, sacred articles, etc., to the management of Basukinath temple for which they have got a rent-free stall within its precincts and have been granted eight bighas of land for growing flowers in addition to the annual Pawana (customary payment) from the temple. Six Jaiswar Kurmi families are the Pawaniyas of Basukinath and each supplies sacred articles for two months in a year by rotation. Six Perghas and two Maithil Brahmins (other than Panda) sell such articles at Basukinath. The Perghas and Maithils totally depend upon pilgrims.

Holy Water Seller: Kankubj

There are a few Kankubj families at Deoghar who have adopted the profession of selling holy water like Gangajal, Saryujal, etc., of different holy rivers of the Hindus. These sellers are in Deoghar for four generations. It is said that being unhappy with the family—first of all of them, Pandit Sadashib Mishra, a saintly man as well as good tabla and flute player, came from Varanasi and met the then Sardar Panda who was pleased with him after listening to his tabla and flute and appointed him as one of the musicians of Baidyanath. In due course Pandit Sadashib Mishra requested the then Sardar Panda to grant him some permanent job so that his progeny may serve Lord Baidyanath. The Sardar Panda granted him the right to sell holy water of different sacred rivers at the Baidyanath Cluster. A rent of Rs. 25 is paid to the Sardar Panda. Currently, eight families are engaged in selling water. The family members are also engaged in secular education and jobs. These eight families belong to Kashi and are of the Shrawani clan but they don't inter-marry and usually they marry in Uttar Pradesh.

They are vegetarian but resemble with the Kankubj Pandas in other cultural facets. They have social relationship with Kankubj Pandas but not with other Pandas.

Gumasta

As already said a Gumasta is he who assists a Panda in helping and guiding a Jajman. The number of Gumastas increases in the months of Magh, Phalgun, Shrawan and Bhadon and decreases during Jeth and Asadh. Gumastas are of two kinds: 1. Permanent, and 2. Seasonal.

1. A permanent Gumasta is he who works round the year with a particular Panda. Permanent Gumastas can be counted on the fingers. Earlier most of the Pandas had a Gumasta. Now-a-days a permanent Gumasta is appointed only in the absence of a male member in the family. Earlier, permanent Gumastas were the status symbol of a Panda but today the scene has changed owing to Pandas' changed, not-so-good financial condition.

Any Brahmin can be a Gumasta provided his behaviour and character is good and has a sound knowledge of the sacred geography of Deoghar and also of the Hindu texts. Generally, familiarity with the family is considered in appointing a Gumasta.

The monthly remuneration of a permanent Gumasta is between Rs. 15 to Rs. 30 with two meals a day. He also gets tips from Jajmans for the noble services rendered to them. Permanent Gumastas also get two pairs of dhotis and kurtas annually—one pair for general use and the other at the time of his annual visit home.

A Gumasta's prime responsibility is to help his Malik in assisting and guiding a Jajman. Whenever his Malik's Jajman comes, he is expected to take care of him. He carries the basket of sacred articles of the Jajman. He also guides Jajmans in the performance of rituals in the absence of his Malik. He also escorts a Jajman to different sacred centres of Deoghar and thus works as a guide also.

He is treated as a family member in his Malik's home. He discharges all kinds of domestic responsibilities of his Malik apart from assisting and guiding a Jajman, on behalf of his Malik. He shares all major responsibilities of his Malik.

2. Seasonal Gumastas are temporary. They assist more than one Panda in a particular season. It is a secondary profession for most of the Gumastas. The Gumastas in this category are more in number than in the category of permanent Gumastas. Seasonal Gumastas are a recent phenomenon. They are usually employed in busy seasons, i.e. during Magh Panchami, Shivratri, Shrawan, etc. Seasonal or temporary Gumastaship provides ample opportunity to the needy of nearby villages. They are also appointed like permanent Gumastas. Sri Tarachand Goswami explains how and why one becomes seasonal or temporary Gumasta : "I hail from Karnibad (a nearby village). I came here as Gumasta only last month (Chait) because of my bad financial condition. I am unable to support my family with the agriculture produce. Another Brahmin of my village, who is also working as a seasonal or temporary Gumasta, encouraged me to adopt this profession for subsistence. Till last year I was working as Pujari (priest) of the Balanand Brahmachari ashram during the slack season but this year another man got appointed there. So I approached Nilkanth Panda who listened to my grief and asked me to attend the temple from the next day. I first of all worshipped Lord Baidyanath and then went to Nilkanth who asked me to assist one of his Jajmans who gave me twenty-five paise. Thus

I started assisting Jajmans but I am still not familiar with all the Pandas. Seasonal or temporary Gumasta's responsibility is very little in comparison to the permanent. They only assist the Panda and his Jajmans in the performing of different rituals of the Baidyanath cluster. Seasonal Gumastas get their remuneration only after their work."

Sikdar

Sikdars are the traditional pawaniyas of Baidyanath and get their annual Pawana from the Sardar Panda on behalf of Baidyanath. They assist a Jajman in offering a goat or buffalo in the Baidyanath cluster. They identify themselves as Kshatriya. Sikdar is their professional title. To slaughter a goat or buffalo in the Baidyanath cluster is their traditional right. This right has been also confirmed by courts of law in several disputes. Numerous examples can be seen in the "Brief" of the Baidynath temple.

Sacred Performances 6

THE SACRED performances at different sacred centres of Deoghar are numerous. They may be discussed here under five broad headings, i.e. Daily Sacred Performances, Monthly Sacred Performances, Annual Sacred Performances, Sacred Performances connected with Kanwar and Sacred Performances connected with vows. We will mainly discuss here the sacred performances observed in the Baidyanath cluster. However, references to the sacred performances at other sacred centres of Deoghar have also been made, whenever necessary.

Daily sacred performances

Daily Sacred Performances refer to all such performances as are observed daily in the Baidyanath cluster by the management of the Baidyanath temple.

Sarkari Puja

It is one of the Daily Sacred Performances by the management in the Baidyanath cluster. It is the first sacred performance of the day. Traditionally, first of all the Sardar Panda worships Lord Baidyanath, no pilgrim or devotee is allowed to worship him, and that's why it is known as Sarkari Puja.

The temple of the Baidyanath is opened in Brahmuhurt (between half past three and four) by the Dwari Panda, Mushrif and a representative of the Sardar Panda. The doors of the temple cannot be opened in the absence of one of the above-mentioned functionaries. Offered flowers, garlands, Belpatra, etc., are removed. Belchandan offered at night is distributed as Gham Chandan in the morning among the present devotees or pilgrims. The time of Sarkari Puja changes from season to season. A Mushrif, representing the Sardar Panda, worships

Lord Baidyanath and then the other deities of the cluster. Silver is offered first of all to Baidyanath which is followed by Panchamrit made of milk, curd, ghee, shakkar and honey. It is followed by the dressing of Baidyanath with a white cloth, Chandan Rori and Axchat, flowers, Belpatra and Dhoop. After this, Baidyanath is given a bath with the holy waters of the sacred rivers and Fulel (scent) is rubbed and Itr (scent) offered to him. Then the Pandas are allowed to offer Kacha Jal (holy water of Chandra Kup) to him while the Mushrif performs Sarkari Puja at the other sacred centres of this cluster. Offering of Kacha Jal continues for an hour or so and then the temple is opened to public till Bhog Arti (midday meal) which is usually performed at 2.30 p.m. If a pilgrim desires to offer Kacha Jal to Lord Baidyanath, he may so do through his Panda.

One of the Gumastas of the Baidyanath temple shouts loudly at 2.30 p.m. to attract the attention of the pilgrims to worship Lord Baidyanath quickly since the temple is to be closed for the Bhoga Arti. The Mushrif removes the offered flowers, garlands, Belpatra, etc. Baidyanath is bathed with Chandra Kup's water and attired in a white cloth. Offering of flowers, garlands, Belpatra, etc., is followed with Bhoga offerings (sweets for meal of Baidyanath). The ingredients of the Bhoga vary from season to season. All then leave and Baidyanath rests till Sringar in the evening. The Mushrif, representing the Sardar Panda assisted by the Pujari, Dwari, Murchhalwala and Chandanwala performs Sringar of Baidyanath after sunset.

Ingredients offered during Bhog Arti are removed and the Mushrif gives Baidyanath a bath and dries him with a silken towel. Chameli oil is then rubbed and a second bath is given to him with the holy waters of different sacred rivers and the Mushrif dries him with another silken towel and offers Itr (scent). Two kilograms of sandal paste is offered to him which is artistically made like a crown by the Mushrif and his assistants. Further, crownlike garlands are offered and Sital Bhog and Pan are offered. Doors are then closed for five minutes. Arti is performed and pilgrims are allowed to have a darshan (view) of Sringar Arti. Similar Sringar Artis are performed at the other sacred centres of the sacred geography of Deoghar.

Shayan Arti (rituals performed at the time of retiring for the day) is performed at 10 p.m. and the temple is closed until next morning. Pilgrims or devotee are not allowed to touch the Lingam after Sringar Arti but the Pandas who have observed a fast on Ekadashi, Purnamasi, etc., are allowed to touch the lingam.

Monthly sacred performances

Monthly Sacred Performances are those which are observed only once in a month by the pilgrims and devotees.

According to the Hindu calendar Purnamasi marks the end of a month. Pilgrims and devotees perform numerous rituals on different Purnamasis.

Most of the pilgrims of Phalgun, Chait and Ashwin Purnamasis of the Hindu calendar are from Bihar and of Baisakh, Jeth, Aghan and Paush are from neighbouring areas. These Purnamasis are locally known as Adhaieya or Botalwala mela. Pilgrims at these occasions fill their bottles on the Purnamasi day at Sultanganj and offer to Baidyanath on Pariwa (first day) or Dooj (second day). A few pilgrims offer holy water of the sacred rivers purchased from holy water sellers on the same (Purnamasi) day. In this way the influx of pilgrims continues for two and a half days and that is why it is known as Adhaieya mela. Further as they bring Gangajal in bottles it is known as Botalwala mela.

Pilgrims of Phalgun Purnamasi worship Baidyanath with Abir (red powder) in addition to the usual sacred articles. Harihar Milan is also performed on this day wherein Baidyanath plays Holi with Krishna. Disciples of the Balanand Brahmachari ashram also come to worship Lord Baidyanath on Phalgun Purnamasi.

Pilgrims of Chait, Baisakh and Jeth generally come here to perform Mundan (first head-shaving ceremony), Vivah (marriage), etc., of their sons and daughters.

Purnamasis of Asadh, Shrawan and Bhadon are of great importance. Pilgrim, in great numbers, from different parts of the country come here to worship Baidyanath. These Purnamasis are marked with the offering of Kanwar, goat and Belpatra after writing Ramnama (name of Rama). Purnamasi of Ashwin is marked with the offering of a goat in addition to other usual articles. In some cases a goat is offered because it is a part of the traditional offerings on lineage or family level. It is also offered in fulfilment of one's vow.

Purnamasi of Aghan and Paush months is of local importance. Most of the Pandas undertake Jajmanika tours during these months. Purnamasi of the Magh month is also of great importance. It is marked with the offerings of Kanwar, Dhoja and Pagri to Baidyanathjee. A few goats are also offered. Pilgrims from different parts of the country come here. A sizable number of the pilgrims also go to worship at Basukinath on the above occasions.

Annual sacred performances

Annual Sacred Performances are those which are observed only once in a year by pilgrim, or devotees or by the temple management in the Baidyanath cluster.

Shrawan

Shrawan is an important month for Deoghar. Pilgrims from all over the Hindu world come to worship Baidyanath. Pilgrims in their thousands pour in touching the peak on every Somwari (Monday) of the Shrawan month.

Pilgrims believe that Baidyanathdham is an important place of pilgrimage during the month of Shrawan and will earn special merit by worshipping Baidyanath in this month. About a hundred pilgrims were interviewed at random during Shrawan and the first half of Bhadon on the basis of an observation schedule and interview guide.

They gave the purposes of their pilgrimage as are shown in the table below.

State	Total No. of Pilgrims	Alone	With family	Average no. of visit	Purpose					
					Business Posting	Religion	Vow: either to take or to fulfil	Importance in Shrawan	Locational consideration	To earn merit
Bihar	52	21	31	2nd	3	11	12	6	14	6
Other than Bihar	48	13	35	2nd	3	6	13	17	1	8

The Table shows that 52 per cent pilgrims are from Bihar and the remaining 48 per cent from different parts of the Hindu world. Most of the pilgrims obviously perfer to worship Baidyanath with their families since 31 out of 52 and 35 out of 48 came with families. Most of the Bihari pilgrims come due to locational considerations wheras non-Biharis come due to the importance of Baidyanath in Shrawan. Similarly 25 per cent pilgrims come either to take a vow or to worship Lord Baidyanath after fulfilment of their vow. The four Mondays, the first and the last day of Shrawan are the important days from pilgrimage and ritual points of view. Some of the pilgrims worship Baidyanath annually on the abovementioned days. Nothing like the Annual Sacred Performances are observed by the management except that the Baba's pat (door) remains open till 10 p.m. or so for the pilgrims and the Sringar Arti is performed around 11 p.m. On these days pilgrims are allowed Sringar darshan till 1 p.m. The temple is opened at 3 a.m. on these days. To worship Lord Baidyanath with the holy water of any sacred river is necessary, therefore pilgrims either bring it with themselves or purchase it from the local holy-water seller. Most of the pilgrims offer Belpatra reciting Ramnama (name of Ram) worship either with Panchoupchar or with Sodsoupchar. A good number of pilgrims believe that to worship Baidyanathjee on Shrawan Purnamasi is a most sacred act. That is why the highest number of pilgrims are found on Shrawan Purnamasi.

Many stalls are erected to sell sacred articles, toys and cosmetics. The sacred zone of Deoghar wears a fairy look during Shrawan and Bhadon. Brahmins from different parts of the country recite the sacred texts, perform Jaap for their Jajmans in the Baidyanath cluster. Sadhoos and many religious organizations present Kirtan, Ramlila, Krishnalila, etc., within the premises of the Baidyanath temple. Different Dals (groups) of the Panda community present religious dramas in their localities and in the premises of the Baidyanath temple also.

A few pilgrims perform Hawan (burning of sandalwood) to mark the completion of all Shastrik (textual) rituals performed at Baidyanathdham. A few Brahmins recite Hariwansh Katha (a Puranik story) for the women pilgrims who come here to be blessed with a child. Most of the pilgrims make sounds like a goat believing that this pleases Baidyanath because King Dexh (father-in-law of Baidyanath) had made such sounds, since then Saivites consider it essential for Shivapujan (worship of Shiva). Generally pilgrims take Sankalpa and give Daxina to Pandas at the end of Baidyanath pooja considering it essential to earn religious merit. Kanwar offering is the special feature of Shrawan and Bhadon. Similarly most of the pilgrims offer Gathbandhan in Shrawan and Bhadon. Kumari Bhoj (to feed unmarried Brahmin girls) is one of the rituals performed by pilgrims during Shrawan. The pilgrims, who are unable to meet the expenses of Kumari Bhoj, give a token amount to their Pandas for Kumari Bhoj. Similarly pilgrims perform Brahmanbhoj to Brahmins in Shrawan. Generally pilgrims deposit a token amount for Brahman Bhojan with their Pandas.

The annual sacred performances of the Pagla Baba Ashram begin from Jhulan Ekadashi of Shrawan and end on Janamashthami in Bhadon. Disciples of the Ashram also worship Baidyanath in the Baidyanath Cluster.

The number of beggars also increases during Shrawan. They reported that they go to Gaya in Ashwin and to Rajgir, Varanasi, Hardwar, Ayodhya, Mathura, etc., during the pilgrim season of the respective places. They move from one place to another because pilgrims need beggars to give alms after performing a ritual and accordingly beggars earn religious merit of pilgrimage by visiting different sacred centres. Pilgrims after worshipping Baidyanath go to worship Basukinath. Kanwarias (pilgrims with Kanwar) also bring Kanwar for Basukinath. Athgauna pilgrims (pilgrims from nearby villages) first of all worship Basukinath and then go to Baidyanathdham. Santhals, Perghas, Dhanuks and Domes of Athgauna also worship Basukinath. Domes simply bow their heads at the main gate of the temple. Santhal, Pergha and Khateri pilgrims and devotees are found more in Basukinath than Deoghar. Unlike Deoghar no annual sacred performances are performed by the management of the Basukinath temple at Basukinath. Here, the temples remain open for pilgrims and devotees till 9 p.m. Thereafter Sringar is performed and the sacred centre of Basukinath remains open for Sringar Darshan till 11.30 p.m. The doors of the temple are opened at 3.30 in the morning. The influx of pilgrims to Basukinath is great, it wears a fair-like look. To give it colour a few cosmetics, toys, sacred articles stalls are erected. A miniature zoo, a small circus party and a theatre company also come to Basukinath in the month of Shrawan to entertain pilgrims and devotees. The theatre company generally stage religious dramas.

Shivratri

Shivratri is one of the Annual Sacred Performances by the management of Baidyanath and Basukinath temples and also by pilgrims and devotees.

It is celebrated throughout the Hindu world on the fourteenth day of the Phalgun Krishna Paxsh believing it to be the consort night of Lord Shiva. It is also celebrated as the Gaddi day (throne day) of the Sardar Panda of Deoghar. He sits on the Gaddi of the Baidyanath temple only once in a year, on this day. A kingly chair is decorated and the Sardar Panda sits on it before performing the marriage and Sringar of Baidyanath. His courtiers also take their respective seats and salute the Sardar Panda. Conventionally, the Sardar Panda is not allowed to sit on this Gaddi on any other day. It is said that one of the Sardar Panda's ancestors became blind by violating this convention.

Shivratri is socially important for the Pandas of Deoghar because they don't solemnize marriages of their daughters or sons before Shivratri in the belief that they are the servants of the Baba and so they should solemnize their marriages only after the marriage of their master.

Different traders from different parts of the country come to sell a variety of products. A few stalls sell only Mauri (marriage cap) since it is a special offering of Shivratri. These stalls wear the look of a fair. Pilgrims from all over the Hindu world come to worship Lord Baidyanath during Shivratri. Most of the pilgrims either bring Ganga Jal with themselves or purchase at Deoghar to offer to Baidyanath. Generally, pilgrims offer Mauri through Sikdar. In some cases Mauri is offered after fulfilment of a vow. Also, vows are generally taken on this day for trouble-free and happy marriages of daughters and in some cases for sons also. Sarkari Puja is performed earlier than on normal days and the temple remains open for pilgrims and devotees till 9 p.m. The marriage of the Baba starts at 10 p.m. and continues till 1 a.m. Five Khachiyas (baskets) containing dhoti, chaddar, dab, axhat-janue, dahi, ghee, doodh, madhu, sindur, rori, bel, dhatura, kasaili, paan, kapur, fal, mithaie and mauri are offered to Baidyanathjee. One of these five Khachiyas comes from the Ghatwal King of Rohini. Previously all the five Khachiyas came from Rohini State but now, after the abolition of zamindari, they are only maintaining the tradition by sending a Khachiya in the belief that Rohini is the in-law's place of Lord Baidyanath. Four Khachiyas come from the temple management. These five offered Khachiyas go to the five Pawanadars of the Baidyanath temple, i.e., Sardar Panda, Diwan, Sikdar, Purohit and Sringari. In 1970 a representative of the Sardar Panda performed the marriage of Lord Baidyanath as the Sardar was indisposed. The throne was not decorated.

The day begins with Lord Baidyanath taking a bath with Ganga Jal. Further each sacred article is offered accompanied by the chanting of mantras. Lastly a Dhoti is offered after wrapping him in the offered towel. Believing that Baidyanath has accepted the dhoti and chaddar, rori, sindur, belpatra, flowers are offered and *Arti* is performed. All those present are asked to vacate the sanctum as it is believed that he is taking his meals. Later they are called in and the Puja for *Charpaher* is performed with the remaining four Khachiyas. One Khachiya's contents are offered for one *paher* Puja of Lord Baidyanath. Sindur is offered to Baidyanath because the dotted line over the Lingam is supposed to be the emblem of Parvatee.

From 1 a.m. the temple remains open for pilgrims and devotees. Pandas also celebrate consort night of Shiva and Parvatee at their respective Gaddis. Some Santhals were also found worshipping Lord Baidyanath during Shivratri.

Pilgrims lead an identical life during Shivratri. Most of them perform Kumari Bhojan and Brahman Bhojan. Most of the pilgrims give alms after Baidyanath Poojan.

Shivratri is also performed by the management of Basukinath temple. The temple is opened earlier on this day for pilgrims after Mangla Arti (Morning prayer) and is closed at 11 p.m. Then the offered articles are removed and the marriage of Lord Shiva performed. The pilgrims and devotees have a darshan. All the articles of a Khachiya which are offered to Lord Baidyanath are also offered to Basukinath and these articles are handled by the temple management. They go to the chief priest of the temple. Most of the pilgrims come here after worshipping Baidyanathjee.

The Perghas of Trikuti also perform the marriage of Trikuteshwarnath. The eldest member of the community, who is elected annually, performs the marriage of Trikuteshwarnath. But not one pilgrim was found here. Similarly devotees of the adjoining village perform Shivratri at Tapovan. Balanad Brahmachari ashram manages the sacred articles on this occasion.

Shivratri is also performed as one of the annual sacred performances at Deo Sangh. Ashramites and other disciples who flock here from all over the country perform Sadhana for a fortnight. Similarly Shivratri is performed as part of annual sacred performances at other sacred centres of Deoghar.

Magh Panchmi

Magh Panchmi, an annual sacred performance, is also known as Sri Panchami and Basant Panchami. The influx of pilgrims increases at this time. The following table gives the approximate number of pilgrims who came to Deoghar during 1960-70 Basant Panchami.

Year	No. of pilgrims during Basant Panchami
1960	26509
1961	24842
1962	17853
1963	18058
1964	27112
1965	25154
1966	29128
1967	22112
1968	21277
1969	26905
1970	24305

Pilgrims from different parts of the country come during Sri Panchami to worship Lord Baidyanath. Believing it as his Tilak day, the Tilak articles come from Rohni since it is his Sasural (in-law's place). *Kanwar* offering is the special feature of this day. Ganga Jal is brought from Sultangang in a *Kanwar* to be offered to Baidyanath and Basukinath. Different Dals (groups) of Pandas celebrate Magh Panchami as Saraswati Puja in their localities. Most of the pilgrims perform Mundan (first hair-cutting ceremony) of their children on this occasion. One pilgrim even came from Nepal to perform Mundan of his son. He said that when his two sons died after a few days of their birth, his mother-in-law took a vow to perform Mundan at Baidyanathdham on Sri Panchmi day if she is blessed with a grandchild. She has also vowed to worship Baidyanathjee with a golden Basha if blessed with a grandson. Most of the Mundans are performed here due to fulfilment of Manokamna.

A pilgrim usually takes a bath in the Shiv Ganga and Sankalpa with the assistance of a Panda, waits in a long queue to worship Baidyanath with the holy water, berries, flowers, Belpatra and abir. (Abir is an essential article of the day because it is a Tilak day as well as the beginning of Basant.) One salutes one's Panda after worshipping Lord Baidyanath. A pilgrim either observes fast or takes Satvic food (vegetarian simple food which may not pollute him). Fast end only after Sringar Arti. Pilgrims are not so particular in offering, holy water from the sacred rivers as only 47 out of 100 offered holy water. Many offered holy water of Chandra Kupa. No special sacred performances are observed in the Baidyanath-Basukinath cluster by the temple management.

Sri Panchami is observed in almost all the Ashrams of Deoghar. An idol of Goddess Sarswati is installed. One of the inmates of Satsang ashram said that they neither discourage nor encourage their disciples in worshipping Lord Baidyanath or in installing the idol of Goddess Sarswati. Sri Panchami is also performed at other sacred centres of Deoghar. Farmers coming to Deoghar at this time bring corn to offer to Lord Baidyanath.

Sali puja

A few pilgrims come annually to worship Lord Baidyanath. This annual visit and annual offerings at the Baidyanath centre is locally known as Sali Puja. Most of the pilgrims are following the family traditions since their ancestors' vows were fulfilled with the grace of Baidyanath. Many pilgrims take vows at Baidyanathdham but only 1 per cent take vows to perform Sali

Puja. Since it is a bit difficult and costly, a few pilgrims who come from zamindar, royal and big business families perform it. Vows are generally taken for a peaceful reign and prosperity in business or in personal life. Sali Puja can be performed on any ordinary or festive day. Those who can afford give Rs. 51 in Daxina to their Pandas with a pair of dhoti and sari and worship Lord Baidyanath with Sodsoupchar. A few perform Sali Puja with Panchoupchar and give Rs. 11 and a pair of sari and dhoti in Puja with Daxina. In the third category of the Sali Puja performers are those pilgrims who offer only flowers, holy water and Re. 1.25 paise in Daxina.

SACRED PERFORMANCES CONNECTED WITH KANWAR

Kanwar offering is an important ritual of Baidyanathdham. Kanwar is a container in which Ganga Jal is stored at Sultanganj, 90 miles away from Deoghar, and is offered to Baidyanath and Basukinath. Kanwar offering is followed with other usual rituals. A Kanwaria (one who brings Kanwar) is respected by other pilgrims since he covers the distance of 90 miles on foot. Kanwar pilgrims come in the maximum number during Magh and Shrawan and specially on Magh Panchami and Shrawan Purnamasi. Kanwar offering is the unique ritual of Deoghar. Mythologically, it is said that Rawan brought holy water from different sacred rivers to worship Lord Baidyanath. So pilgrims are also expected to offer Kanwar to get their manokamna (desires) fulfilled. Kanwar of Magh differs from the Kanwar of Shrawan, so they are being discussed separately.

Kanwars offered to Baidyanathjee during Magh are of provincial nature as most of the Kanwarias essentially belong to Bihar.

Kanwars are of different kinds and structure but broadly they can be classified under the following categories:

Khara kanwar

Kanwar and Kanwaria remain khara (standing) till it is not offered to Baidyanath or in some cases to Basukinath. A Khara Kanwaria covers the distance of 90 miles within 24 hours without taking rest or food. Khara Kanwar is offered either for or after fulfilment of a vow related to the birth of a child of either sex, to settle the marriages of daughters or grand-daughters or to win a complicated court case. Most of the Khara Kanwaria appoint two or three men to carry Kanwar by turns. These men may be his relatives, friends or hired men. Khara Kanwar must not be changed from one shoulder to another until it is offered.

Baitha kanwar

It can be placed at any holy place according to convenience of the pilgrim. Majority of the pilgrims prefer to offer Baitha Kanwar. The total time in covering the distance of 90 miles differs from one group to another. Most of the pilgrims offer Baitha Kanwar for more than a year, so they don't feel any trouble in covering this distance.

Dakbam kanwar

A Kanwaria who offers Dakbam Kanwar neither stays nor transfers Kanwar before offering the stored holy water to Baidyanath. He neither takes assistance of any other person nor takes any food until the Kanwar is offered. It is offered to save anyone from long illness or to win a complicated court case, or for the resolution of any other complicated problem. Pilgrims generally cover the distance within twenty-four hours.

Phalhari kanwar

It is similar to Baitha Kanwar except that pilgrims offering Baitha Kanwar eat grains whereas the pilgrims of this category eat fruits.

Pilgrims offering Kanwars in Magh usually bring paddy with them. They throw it on the roof of the Baidyanath temple before worshipping him. One of the pilgrims said that Indian agriculture is a gamble with the monsoon, that is why they offer him whatever they get from him considering the return from the land as his gift.

Kanwar pilgrims have a special privilege to offer Kanwar. They can offer Kanwar even when the temple is closed. Conventionally a temple is opened if any Kanwar pilgrim approaches, even after its closure.

Kanwar during Shrawan

Kanwars offered during Shrawan are of all-India importance as Kanwarias flock in from different parts of the Hindu world.

Randomly selected hundred Bams (Kanwar pilgrims) of different age and sex groups with the help of an interview guide have been interviewed. They consisted of 62 Marwari and 38 Deshwal Kanwar pilgrims. Among these five are *Dome* by caste and one is a tribal of Santhal Pargana. Pandas and local people classify Bams into two categories on the basis of their native places. Those coming from other States are known as Marwari Bams and those from Bihar are known as Deshwal Bams. Bams of Shrawan were predominantly Marwaris but now-a-days Deshwal Bams are in an overwhelming majority during Shrawan. Two Deshwals offered Bam Kanwar. Three Marwaris and one Deshwal offered Khara Kanwar. Twenty Marwaris and eleven Deshwals offered Phalahari Kanwar. Twenty-five Marwaris and twenty Deshwals offered Baitha Kanwar. Six Marwaris and three Deshwals offered Somwari Kanwar. Sixty-two Marwaris and thirty-six Deshwals offered Kanwar with the assistance of Panda whereas one Deshwal and one Marwari offered without help. Fifty-seven Marwaris and thirty Deshwals offered Kanwar to Lord Baidyanath because of Manokamna Lingam. One Marwari and four Deshwals undertook Kanwar pilgrimage as a picnic. Twelve Marwaris and twelve Deshwals offered Kanwar to earn merit in the next life. Most of the Bams offer Kanwar more than once. Fifty-six Marwaris and twenty Deshwals also offered Kanwar at Basukinath.

Structure of kanwar

Kanwar of Shrawan differs from the Kanwar of Magh in structure. Shrawan Kanwars are well decorated and are comparatively lighter than Magh Kanwars. Shrawan Kanwars differ in size from Bam to Bam whereas Magh Kanwars are mostly of one size. Magh Kanwars can carry the baggage of Bams whereas Shrawan Kanwars cannot and the luggage is carried by the coolies.

Shrawan Kanwars are similar to Magh Kanwars in kind. Bams of Magh generally eat chura and dahi whereas Sharwan

Bams take arwa rice and gram pulse, and don't take onion and garlic. Somwari Kanwars are offered only in Shrawan. It may be any kind of Kanwar but it must be offered on Somwar (Monday), hence it is known as Somwari Kanwar.

Life of Bams

A Bam takes Sankalpa after taking a bath in the Ganga at Sultanganj to offer holy water to Lord Baidyanath and also in some cases of Basukinath. One becomes a Bam just after taking Sankalpa. They address one another as Bam. In no case can one address another by name otherwise one will have to take a fresh Sankalpa for which he is required to take a bath at Sultanganj. When a mother and son or husband and wife come to perform Kanwar ritual the local Pandas (at Sultanganj) strongly warn pilgrims not to call each other by name but as Bam.

There are several Chattis (rest-houses) on the way where Bams stay for the night. Most of the Bams prepare Satwik or Hawish food at these Chattis. Phalhari Bams take only fruits. A Kanwar pilgrim is always careful in avoiding any action that may pollute another Kanwar pilgrim. He sings devotional songs throughout the pilgrimage. Dholakias move with a group of Bams. They sing Bhajans (devotional songs) and sometimes, out of devotion, dance also.

Purificatory rules are observed during the period. All the relevant rules of Hinduism are observed by a Kanwar pilgrim.

Personal purification

A Bam is always particular about personal purification. He sings devotional songs to keep himself pure. He sprinkles Ganga jal over head and body after Sauch and before taking Kanwar. He keeps a bottle of Ganga jal for this purpose. He bathes before taking Kanwar in case of stay at any Chatti during the day or at night.

Dress

Purificatory rules are observed regarding clothes. They are changed after Sauch (calls of nature) and after all such actions which may pollute them. There is similarity in dress among the

Bams. They wear orange-coloured under-wears, vests and Ramnama Chaddars or a towel and the female Bams wear an orange coloured sari and blouse. Orange-coloured clothes are used in the belief that Bams are Sanyasis and Kanwar offering is Tapasya (meditation). The clothes worn are new and are prepared only for this occasion.

Food

It is important for a Bam not to pollute himself. One may be an intellectual, businessman, labourer, etc. but as soon as one becomes a Bam one has to observe all the purificatory rules specially of food. Bams take only Satwik food. They don't take onion or garlic. Bams take only Arwa rice. Usna rice is not allowed. Intoxication is strictly forbidden during the period. Bams neither smoke nor chew tobacco, but Ganja and Bhaang are allowed, these are considered Prasad of Baidyanath.

Observance of celibacy

Male pilgrims take a vow to offer Kanwar accompanied by wife or vice versa. In such cases celibacy is observed till the Kanwar is offered at Baidyanathdham. Most of the Bams of this category vow for a child. This is why they don't observe any sex restriction after worshipping Lord Baidyanath since they believe to be blessed with a child with the grace of Lord Baidyanath, and in this case it matters little whether they offer Kanwar at Basukinath or not. If by chance a female pilgrim menstruates it does not pollute her rather it is considered as his Prasad.

Offering of kanwar

A Bam does five Parikarmas after entering the Baidyanath temple and bows his head before the deities of the cluster and meets with his Panda. He sings devotional songs while doing circumbulation. He keeps his Kanwar with the Panda and goes to take a bath in the Shivganga. He worships the Shivganga before the bath. Arghya or Sastang Dandwat is performed according to one's vow. A pilgrim comes to his Panda who assists him in performing Sankalpa and the pilgrim goes to offer holy water to Baidyanath and it is followed by Hawan,

Brahaman Bhojan, Kumari Bhojan, Gathbandan, Pataka, goat, etc., according to one's convenience and nature of vow.

Post-Bam period

After offering Kanwar to Lord Baidyanath and to Basukinath one enters a post-Bam phase and no longer is he known as Bam. Bams now address one another by name and take food of their choice and lead a normal life.

SACRED PERFORMANCES CONNECTED WITH VOW

Mundan

Pilgrims perform Mundan (first hair-cutting ceremony) of their children at the Baidyanath and Basukinath Sacred Cluster. Pilgrims pay either 75 paise in the office of the Baidyanath temple or Re. 1.25 in the office of Dharmraxhni Society to perform Mundan on the premises of the Baidyanath temple and at Singh Darwaja of the Basukinath temple respectively. A few paise with Arwa rice and shaved hairs are given as Neg (customary gift) to Dome or Domin who sit near the Kesh Kund. To take Neg is the hereditary right of these Domes or Domins. A child is given a bath with the water of the Neer Kund. A Brahmin, who is Gumasta of a Panda, allows water to be taken from the Kund after realising some Daxina. The holy water offered to Lord Baidyanath is collected in this Kund. A child is given a bath in the Shivganga and then is made to worship Baidyanath. A good number of Mundans are performed on different monthly and annual sacred performance days. Most of the Mundans are performed here due to Manokamna. Most of the parents come in fulfilment of the vows taken to be blessed with a child or for other mundane purposes. It is also believed that a child also gets blessings from Baidyanath for peaceful and prosperous life. In a few cases pilgrims perform Mundan simply because they happen to have come to Deoghar.

Vivah

Marriage is another important sacred performance performed at the Baidyanath cluster by pilgrims. People from all over Bihar, Nepal and West Bengal come here to perform marriages in Phalgun, Chait, Baisakh, Jeth and Asadh. Of these Jeth is a more important month for marriages. Anyone coming to perform marriage pays Rs. 31. 25 to Dharmraxhni Society to register the marriage. A receipt is issued and it is a valid document in a court of law. Marriages are performed within the temple premises and most of the pilgrims worship Baidyanath with Panchoupchar just after Sindur dan (putting of vermillion in the hair parting). Marriages are performed here in the belief that couples would be blessed by Baidyanathjee with a happy and prosperous conjugal life. In a random interview it was found that 20 such marriage pilgrims were from West Bengal, one from Nepal, one from Rajasthan and seventy-eight from Bihar. Of the hundred, only ten had taken a vow to celebrate the marriage of their child at the Baidyanath sacred centre. The rest of the marriages were performed either due to economic or social reasons. Only ten said that they are performing the marriage under supervision of Lord Baidyanath. The rest gave vague answers. About five hundred and fifyseven marriages are performed annually at the Baidyanath sacred centre (calculated on the basis of the Register of Dharmraxhni Society) on the basis of the marriage register from March 1960 to March 1970.

Gathbandan and dhaja

Offerings of Gathbandan and Dhaja are part of the rituals performed by pilgrims at Deoghar. Gathbandan is popularly known as Pagri. It is made of Lal Ekranga (red cloth) by a section of the Dariharey Pandas of Deoghar. The length of the Pagri is 308 feet. It is so lengthy because it is tied between Kalash of Baidyanath and Parvatee temple. Dhaja is also prepared by some men. Pilgrims are required to deposit Re. 1.37 for Pagri offering and 62 paise for Dhaja offering to the temple management which provides a Dhanuk to hang Dhaja or Pagri. Generally the Dhanuk throws the Pagri after fixing one end at Baidyanath Kalash to the pilgrims who carry it to the Parvatee temple themselves to tighten the other end personally. Pagri and Dhaja are offered throughout the year but their number touches the peak point during Ramnavmi, Shivratri, Sri Panchmi and Shrawan Purnima. In some cases

Dhaja or Pagri is offered either after or for the fulfilment of Manokamna. These two are also offered at Baidyanath.

Goat offering

Goat is offered as part of a ritual at the Baidyanath and Basukinath cluster by pilgrims. It is offered at the Parvatee sacred centre at the Baidyanath cluster because Tripurasundari and Mahesh Mardan who are enshrined with Parvatee, Gayetri, Mahakalvairab, Bagladevi, Anand Vairab, Tara and Kali of the Baidyanath cluster are non-vegetarians. Weekly offerings (on Tuesdays) of goat are made at Kali sacred centre of Bhitar Khand (residence of the Sardar Panda) by Sikdar on behalf of the Sardar Panda to complete the weekly puja of Kali. Goats are offered at a fixed place at Basukinath, i.e. Yup. Yups are worshipped like a deity by pilgrims and devotees. Goats are fixed and slaughtered at this Yup. Pilgrims are required to pay 87 paise to temple management at both the places and a few coins as Neg to Sikdar who does the slaughtering. First of all, a pilgrim or devotee sprinkles water on a goat. This is believed to be a sacred bath for purifying the goat. Then the goat is offered to the deity like other sacred articles. A Panda chants a few mantras. The goat is brought outside facing towards the deity. One man tightly holds back the legs of the goat and Sikdar slaughters it in a single stroke. The head profusely bleeding and a piece of the flesh are offered to the deity in the belief that the deity concerned would consume it. The remaining part of the sacrificed goat is considered as the Prasad of the deity. Goats are offered as part of Sali Puja or Manokamna ritual.

Dharna

Dharna is another important ritual performed by pilgrims at Baidyanathjee. Pilgrims call it a kind of Tapasya (meditation). Dharna is exclusively performed for the fulfilment of a desire. A Dharnadhari is a common sight within the temple premises. Generally a Dharnadhari sits in the back portico of the Baidyanath temple. A Dharnadhari considers Lord Baidyanath as civil court and Basukinath as criminal court for performing Dharna rituals. It means a Dharnadhari expects quicker results at Basukinath than Deoghar. A Dharnadhari first of all contacts his Panda who manages everything for him and assists his Jajman in taking Sankalpa. Further the Dharnadhari sits in Dharna. He spends all his time in reading the sacred texts or in singing devotional songs. He worships Lord Baidyanath in the morning like other pilgrims and devotees and also performs Sringar Arti like others. He does not eat anything before the Sringar Arti. He takes either Satwik food or only fruits. If Lord Baidyanath appears in his dream in the course of the Dharna, he also suggests means for the fulfilment of Manokamna but if Parvatee appears in the dream then it is supposed that the Dharna cannot be fulfilled. In some cases Dharnadharis take a fresh Sankalpa until Lord Baidyanath appears in dream. A Dharna can be started on any day. Pilgrims from different parts of the country come here to perform the Dharna ritual.

The Sacred Complex 7

TRANSFORMATION IN THE SACRED GEOGRAPHY

THE SACRED geography of Deoghar covers an area of twentynine miles. It also includes Basukinath. The extent of transformation can be discussed in historical perspective at the level of sacred centres. The sacred centres of the Baidyanathjee cluster have been discussed earlier.

At present there are twentysix sacred centres of different deities in this cluster. But, according to Mr. Brooke (Brief—judgements of different courts on different issues regarding the Baidyanath temple compiled together are known as *Brief-1889*), there were only eighteen sacred centres. The sacred centres constructed after Brooke's report (1889) are Savitri, Gaurishankar, Narmdeshwar, Tara and Mansa. These five sacred centres have been constructed by different Sardar Pandas of the Baidyanath temple and have extended the sacred geography of this cluster.

Apart from the extension of the sacred geography there are a few cases of negligence also. The sacred centres of Phagdoor and Nathbari have been completely neglected. At Phagdoor, a hotel is being run by one of the Pandas of Deoghar and the hotel remains closed during Harihar Milan. Nathbari is completely neglected and is in a dilapidated condition. All the sacred centres of the Harlajori, Ravan Kund and the Jagaruth-mandir-Mansingh cluster are neglected. These sacred centres were of all-India importance but have now been brought down to the level of local importance. The sacred centres of the Deo Sangh-Balanand cluster are of recent origin except the Tapovan and are of all-India importance. Similarly, the sacred centres of the Satsang-Nandan hill cluster except for the Nandan hill are of recent origin and are of all-India importance. Sacred centres of the Kalimandir-Basukinath cluster were of regional importance but now they have gained an all-India status. The establishment of different Ashrams in the last few decades has also extended the sacred geography of Deoghar. These Ashrams were established because at Baidyanath are enshrined Baidyanath as well as their Guru. This endorses the view that these Ashrams feel the impact of Baidyanathjee and have considerable interaction between the sacred centres of the Baidyanathjee cluster of Ashrams.

The sacred clusters which were under the control of non-Brahmins are now under the control of Brahmins, such as Basukinath.

In the beginning of this century Basukinath was not so important for the pilgrims but as soon as it was linked by a road, many pilgrims coming to Deoghar started visiting Basukinath also. Now a majority of the pilgrims going to Deoghar also go to Basukinath.

Some of the sacred centres which were under the control of Brahmins are now under the control of non-Brahmins, such as the sacred centres of the Baiju-Sitla cluster, Deosangh-Balanand sacred cluster and of Trikuti and Basukinath sacred segments. The custodian of the Baiju sacred centre was a Panda and it was a vegetarian sacred centre whereas the current custodian is a Gowala by caste and *bali* (sacrifice of a goat) is offered here. Similarly Tapovan was under the custody of the local Panda and the sacred centres were vegetarian whereas the present custodian is a disciple of Balanand and the centres have been transformed into a non-vegetarian sacred centre.

Another interesting feature of the transformation in the sacred geography of Deoghar is that the earlier deities were symbolically represented and such representations were worshipped but now the Gurus of the Ashrams are also worshipped in their physical form.

TRANSFORMATION IN THE SACRED SPECIALISTS

The sacred specialists of Deoghar have considerably changed and are still in the process of change. The sacred specialists used to be named after the various manifestations of God or professional specialisation, *mulgram*, lineage, individual characteristics, etc. But today young sacred specialists, prefer to name their children after film actors and actresses like Dilip Kumar, Rajesh Khanna, Meena Kumari, Helen and so on as perhaps for literary figures.

Similarly the sacred specialists had a single residential pattern strictly within the sacred zone but now they are extending their residences to the secular zone. Accommodation for the pilgrims is no more a part of their residential building. The typical houses of the sacred specialists are a matter of the past and now the houses are being constructed in the Western style, like the houses of the secular zone.

A considerable change in the food habits has also occurred. They used to take rice during the day and *chura dahi* at night but now *chura dahi* has been replaced by wheat and bread and vegetables are taken in the evening. Taboos relating to food have also changed. The sacred specialists belonging to a particular caste group did not dine with the sacred specialists of other caste groups. Now they not only dine with each other they also eat at restaurants. A considerable change in their hobbies has been also found: they no longer have any interest in birds, wrestling, music, etc., they would rather spend their leisure in earning some money by rendering services other than those of their profession of priestcraft or in watching movies. As regards change in the dress, they can be seen assisting Jajmans in pyjamas. They also wear sleeping suits, *lungis*, etc., which were once taboo for them. Their ceremonial dress has also undergone a change. Bridegrooms are found in suits or in trousers and shirts, so is the case with the *Yagopawit*, *Mundan* and with the members of a Barat (marriage party). The womenfolk can also be seen attending school, college and social occasions in garments of the latest fashion. They no longer wish to become mothers at an early age, and care little for social criticism. They also do not observe most of the taboos associated with pregnancy. They are now orienting their children more for secular jobs than for their traditional profession of priestcraft. Transformation in the age of marriage and the marriage customs has also been found. Maithils and Kankubjs like Chakravartys are also marrying off their daughters after puberty. Women's dominant role in settling the marriage is also vanishing fast due to introduction of dowry system and also because of the fact that the marriages are being settled outside the sacred city.

The daily life of the sacred specialists of Deoghar has also undergone change. The younger generation wake up about seven in the morning without uttering the name of Baidyanath. They go to the temple after taking tea and breakfast at a restaurant. During the evening hours, instead of assisting their Jajmans in performing *sringar* rituals, most of them are found at the cinema halls. The younger generation is mostly in favour of secular education and secular jobs. The social interaction at intra- and inter-group levels has also undergone transformation. Most of them are not inclined to continue in the profession of priestcraft. Their Jajmans also advise them to take up secular jobs. This has had a considerable effect on the Panda-Jajman relationship. *Milnewala Panda* is a new phenomenon among the sacred specialists of Deoghar. It is a class and not a caste. Milnewala Pandas are more among Maithils than among the remaining two groups. Though they all consider it a social evil none is in a position to check it. The Pandas have their traditional jajmans but the Milnewala Pandas do not have any such Jajmans. A Milnewala Panda is recognizable from a distance. He can be termed as a pilgrim-hunter. He is to be found at different railway stations, bus stands, important road crossings always on the lookout for pilgrims. He is wise enough to understand that you are not decided who your Panda is and is quick enough to introduce himself to you as your Panda. Many of the pilgrims go to them just for convenience sake because they are always assisted in performing short-cut rituals and therefore, are also charged smaller fees compared to what is charged by the traditional Panda. It is a recent development but is developing fast just because of the convenience of both the parties, that is, short-cut ritual, lower charges, saving of time and energy for the pilgrim and a good earning through such jajmans for the Milnewala Panda.

TRANSFORMATION IN THE SACRED PERFORMANCES

The extent of transformation in the case of the sacred performance is not so visible as is in the case of sacred geography or sacred specialists. However, the transformation in the daily sacred performances is noticeable. Earlier the *sarkari puja* and *sringar* were performed by the *sardar panda* but now are being performed by a Brahmin appointed and paid for this work. The sacred articles offered during these performances have also undergone considerable change. Monthly sacred performances were performed by the regional pilgrims but now a good number of these performances have acquired national patronage. A few sacred performances are now being performed at the Baidyanath precincts more because of the secular nature than sacred nature, for example, the number of marriages performed at the Baidynath sacred centre is more owing to the secular purpose than to sacred performances. Marriages performed here are, in some cases, the result of love. The increasing influx of pilgrims also contributes to the transformation in the sacred performances. Interaction among the disciples of different Ashrams of Deoghar and the pilgrims has been widely observed. This also contributes to the transformation of the sacred performances.

BAIDYANATH IN SHIV PURAN

A description of Chaturthkoti Rudra Sanhita-Dwadashjyotirlingam.
According to Sutajee :

> Nobody can count the whole lingam. The universe is full of lingams. All the Tirthas are full of lingams. Everything is contained in lingams. People attain success only after worshipping the figures of those lingams. In Saurashtra there is a lingam of Somnath; in Shree Shails, the lingam of Mallikarjun; Mahakal is in Ujjain and that of the Parmeshwar is in Onkar. Kedareshwar is established in Varanasi and the lingam of Trayambak is on the banks of the Gomati river. The Baidyanath (lingam) is in Chitabhumi, Nagesh is in Daruka forest and in Setubadh there is the lingam of Dhurmesha Shiva. The person who worships the above twelve Shivalingams first thing in the morning, will find all his desires fulfilled. After worshipping these Jyotirlingams troubles will vanish and the person will get salvation in both the worlds, that is, Mrityaloka and Swarga (Heaven). One should make the offerings to Lord Shiva with great

zeal because one is able to wash away all sins in doing so . . . .
Even among the Rakshasas Lord Shiva has been worshipped and meditated upon by Ravan on top of the Kailash mountain. Ravan was an authority among the giants, full of pride and commanding respect. However Shiva could not be propitiated in such a short while. And so, again he meditated with greater concentration at the sacred corner of the southern Himalaya. He dug a deep pit and lit a sacrificial fire and performed a *havan* asking Shiva to present himself. He suffered the harsh summer season, the biting winter season and the heavy rainfall and performed three kinds of *havans*. Even so Lord Shiva refused to comply with Ravan's request because the latter was a demon. Then Ravan began chopping off his own heads one by one to offer to Shiva and in this way he cut off nine heads and offered them. Only one head remained and at this stage Shiva appeared before him. He restored all the nine heads of Ravan and conferred on him great powers and fulfilled all his desires. Then Ravan prostrating himself at Shiva's feet said in a humble voice "O Lord Shiva, foremost among the Gods, please continue to be pleased with me. I shall bring you to Lankapuri (the kingdom of Ravan) and I hope you shall fulfil my mission. . . .
Lord Shiva was at his wits' end when he found out what Ravan's mission was. And He hailed Ravan as the chief of the demons. He further said that He was pleased with this display of affection. So He gave one of the best Jyotirlingams to him to take home. But He cautioned him that if he put down the lingam at any place on earth while on his way, the lingam would be established there. Ravan started for his home taking along the Shivalingam. On the way Ravan felt the urgent need to relieve himself (this was an illusion created by Lord Shiva himself). He saw a *gopa* (milkman) and requested him to hold the lingam while he relieved himself. The gopa could not carry the heavy weight of the lingam and he set it down. Thus Baidyanatheshwaran Jyotirlingam was established and became famous by the name of Baidyanatheshwar—One who fulfilled any

wish and forgave one's sins. It is famous by the name of Baidyanatheshwar in the three *lokas* (worlds). Ravan returned home and narrated the whole story to his wife. Indra, Brahma, Vishnu came there and worshipped Shiva with great zeal. On seeing Lord Shiva the gods who were present bowed before Him calling Him Baidyanatheshwar and then started back for heaven.

The sage asked Sutajee to narrate in detail the whole story of that sacred place after Ravan and other gods had left. Accordingly, Sutajee said :

Ravan went to his home and narrated the whole story to his wife. Having learnt this she became very pleased. And Indra with other *Deotas* (gods) became tormented and discussed among themselves about the inhuman character of Ravan, a monster in disguise. They stated that Ravan had now got the boon of Lord Shiva and would trouble them. Then they called on Narad and narrated the whole story. Narad consoled them and assured them that he would make his best efforts for their welfare. After that Narad went to Ravan. He praised him for his great achievement and asked him to narrate the story of his achievement. Ravan became pleased and narrated the whole matter before Narad saying that he would conquer the three *lokas*. Narad laughed at this and told Ravan to follow his advice saying that he should not be so confident to get the boon of Lord Shiva. Narad said that the Lord Shiva was not truthful because he was always in a drunken mood. . . . So one could not believe in him so confidently.
Ravan also started for his place with this intention in mind that he would conquer the three *lokas*—by the grace of Lord Shiva. And nobody could beat him so long as he had the sacred weapon given by Lord Shiva.

Thus, if a person listens to the story of the Mahatam of Baidyanatheshwar his sins will be washed away.

Conclusion 8

THE SACRED complex in Deoghar has been broadly discussed in its three aspects, namely sacred geography, sacred specialists and sacred performances. The nature and extent of transformation in the sacred complex have also been discussed.

The sacred geography of Deoghar has been divided into sacred and secular zones on the basis of the predominance of the sacred and secular elements. The boundaries of the sacred zone, however, cut across municipal limits of Deoghar town. In other words, the boundaries of the sacred zone overlap the boundaries of the secular zone. As mentioned earlier the sacred geography of Deoghar covers an area of twenty-nine miles which includes Basukinath.

There are two sacred sub-zones, viz., Deoghar and Basukinath, which are further divided into a number of segments. The Deoghar sub-zone has been classified into Baidyanath, Harlajori, Rohini and Tapovan segments and Basukinath into Trikuti and Basukinath. Each segment is further divided into clusters which enshrine various sacred centres.

In each cluster old and new sacred centres are found. Old sacred centres are those which have textual reference.

There are twenty-nine sacred centres in the Baidyanathjee cluster of which only two, i.e., Baidyanath and Parvatee, have reference in the Shiva Puran. The sacred centres have been constructed by the generous pilgrims, devotees and the sacred specialists of Deoghar. In one cluster both vegetarian and non-vegetarian deities have been accommodated, i.e., in the Baidyanathjee cluster the Baidyanath sacred centre is vegetarian whereas in the Parvatee, Tara, Kali, etc., are non-vegetarian. The sacred centres have also been discussed in terms of pilgrim patronage.

It has been noticed that the sacred specialists of Deoghar belong to three sub-castes of Brahmins, i.e., Maithil, Radhi and Kankubj. They are organized into Gotra and Mulgram. The surnames associated with individual characteristics and lineage have also been discussed. Sacred specialists reside close to the main shrine. Maithil, Radhi and Kankubj occupy different localities.

The dialect of the Panda is different from the local dialect. Though the Pandas come from three different linguistic groups their professional dialect is one. The Pandas of Deoghar with some exceptions in the Kankubj area have similar food habits. They are all non-vegetarian. The entire life-cycle of the Panda is governed by a deep faith in Baidyanathjee.

The sacred specialists have Jajmani system, with their pilgrims and with their associates.

There are two kinds of sacred performances—Sarkaripuja, offered by the temple management, and the other offered by the pilgrims. These performances vary in details and content not only according to season and occasion but also according to the purpose.

A typical feature of the sacred performances at Deoghar is the offering of Kanwar. It is believed that Baidyanathjee is the Manokamnalingam.

While going over the nature and extent of transformation in the sacred complex in Deoghar it has been found that there are at present twentysix sacred centres in the Baidyanathjee cluster whereas Mr. Brooke has referred to only eighteen in 1869. Increase or decrease in the patronage of the sacred centres has also been studied. Establishment of different Ashrams has extended the sacred geography of Deoghar. Changes in the management of a shrine have also been noticed. Gurus of different Ashrams are being worshipped as God.

There has been transformation in the surname, residence pattern, food habits and dress of the Pandas. The nature and extent of the transformation is not so visible in the sacred performances as it is in the sacred geography and sacred specialists.

II

In the preceding section a summary has been given. Now we come to the conclusions arrived at and the results of the hypotheses tested in the present study.

The sacred complex of Deoghar represents in a microcosm, the Indian civilization, in other words, the sacred complex of Deoghar represents unity in diversity. Although the sacred centres belong to various sects, viz. Vaishnava, Shakti and Shaiva, in all these there is a Shivalingam. The predominance of the cult Baidyanath is, however, noticeable from the fact that all the sacred centres in Deoghar follow the major festivals, particularly Shivaratri observed in the Baidyanath temple.

Similarly, there is an overall homogeneity among the sacred specialists of Deoghar in spite of their caste heterogeneity. Brahminical and non-brahminical specialists represent generally great and little traditions respectively. The latter are however basically oriented in the little tradition but they operate with the former almost at equal level.

The sacred complex of Deoghar unites the people of Hindu faith all over the world irrespective of the nationl boundaries. Pilgrims from Nepal or Bangladesh lead the same life as the Indian pilgrims.

Pilgrims from different political, social and economic groups who worship Lord Baidyanath and identify themselves with the same God and share in common all the sacred performances prescribed by the sacred tradition of Deoghar and also share the common cultural knowledge transmitted by the sacred specialists.

The sacred complex of Deoghar provides a unique opportunity for the low and the high to mingle with each other and to lead an identifical life. They do not discriminate among themselves. While offering Kanwar all—whether from a scheduled tribe or a scheduled caste or a high caste—wear similar dress and have similar food habits and way of life. Thus the sacred complex of Deoghar is a uniting agent which brings different nationalities, classes, castes and tribes together.

As stated throughout, the sacred specialists and the pilgrims have shown enough evidence of the fact that the sacred complex in Deoghar acts as a balancing force between orthodoxy and modernity to the extent of helping continuity in the tradition of sacred performances while itself accepting substantially to the changes in dress, food habits and housing patterns.

The sacred specialists of a Hindu place of pilgrim visit their Jajmans periodically in different parts of the country to collect Dakshina and to consolidate the Panda-Jajman relationship thereby sustaining the faith of their Jajmans in Lord Baidyanath.

When a Jajman makes a pilgrimage to Baidyanath he stays with his Pandajee. This Panda-Jajman relationship helps perpetuate the sacred tradition of Baidyanath in depth and extend in space.

It may also be noted here that although the sacred complex of Deoghar resembles the sacred complex of Gaya, Janakpur and Rajgir, it has a certain special feature which marks it from all others. While Gaya is a place noted for a particular kind of ritual (Pind-dan) Janakpur is a place which Vaishnava adore most on account of its being the birthplace of Sita, Rajgir has Buddhist, Jain and Brahminic importance of a general nature. Deoghar stands apart in the sense that here is enshrined the *Manokamanalingam* which fulfils the desires (Manokamana) of the devotees. Therefore, the devotees, visiting Deoghar make a pilgrimage for very mundane things—birth of a child, marriage, cure of a disease, success in elections and for a variety of worldly objects, of secular nature. Perhaps, nowhere else sacred is used so conspicuously and cultivated for secular purposes. This indeed presents a case that in Indian civilization it is hard to draw a line between sacred and secular. And this I think is the main finding of the present study in the sacred complex of Deoghar.

PART TWO

RAJGIR

Rajgir
Historical Baidyanathdham

9

RAJGIR, enjoying historical and religious importance, is situated in Nalanda district of Bihar. It is located 90 km south-east of Patna (capital of Bihar) and 60 km north-east of Gaya (a religious city). According to the 1961 Census the total population of Rajgir is 9033. It is spread over an area of 5 square km. It is a developing township. The people in general are simple and kind. The men-folk generally don simple Dhoti and Kurta and the women are clad in saree and blouse. A few of them, of course, young can be seen in fashionable dresses. Currently, the growing township is gaining prominence due to Buddhism and Jainism.

The history of Rajgir is glorious. It was the capital of Magadh and was known by more than one name of which mention may be made of Vasumati, Brahdrathapura, Grivraja, Kusagrapura and Rajgriha. The name of Vasumati is found in the Ramayana, probably owes its origin to the mythical king Vases, a son of Brahma, to whom the foundation of the city is traditionally ascribed. The name of Brahdrathapura is reminiscent of King Brihadratha, a forefather of the famous king Jarasandh and the founder of a dynasty. The physical features of the area—hills on all sides—has given it the name of Grivraja (enclosure of hills). The name Kusagrapura is found in the literature of Hieun Tsang and in the Jaina and in some Sanskrit or Buddhist texts. Hein Tsiang says that it means the city of superior grass and has reference to the fragrant grass growing all round. It owes its origin to King Kusagra, the successor of Brihadratha. The name Rajgrih or royal abode is an appropriate designation of a place that has remained the capital of Magadh for centuries. Hieun Tsiang, however, implies that this name was strictly applicable only to the new

Rajgriha to the north of hill grit area. The hills that enclose Rajgriha are traditionally five in number. Their enumeration differs in different texts. The Mahabharata, for example, gives their name as Vaibhara, Varaha, Vrishabha, Rishigiri and Chityaka, at another place the text specifies them as Pondara, Vipula, Varakaka, Chityaka and Matanga. The Pali text has another set of names, Vaibhara, Pandara, Vipula, Gridhkuta and Rishigiri. The present names are Vaibhara, Vipula, Ratna, Chatta, Saita, Udaya, Gridhkutta, and Sona, their origin being due to Jainas. It is very difficult to identify the modern names with their ancient representation.

It is stated in the Ramayana that Grivraja was founded by Vasu the fourth son of Brahma, the Creator. For a long time after this tradition is silent about the city till we come to the days of the Kurukshetra war, when Brihadratha, it is said, established himself at this place and became the progenitor of the Brahdratha dynasty known after his name. One of his successors was the famous Jarasandh who is said to have gained reputation as the most powerful king of his time. He had a matrimonial alliance with Kansa, the ruler of Mathura and maternal uncle of Lord Krishna. When Krishna killed Kansa for his misdeeds, Jarasandh marched on Mathura to exterminate the tribesmen of Krishna but was repulsed. After this Krishna visited Grivraja with the Pandva brothers Bhima and Arjuna. Acting on his advice, Bhima killed Jarasandh in a duel. The dynasty of Jarasandh, however, continued to rule till later times.

Coming to more historical times when the Buddha was practising his law, we find a new dynasty with Bimbisara as the king (543-491 B.C.) ruling over Magadh. He was one of the four powerful kings ruling over northern India, the other three being Prasenjit of Kosala, Udyana of Vatsa and Prodyota of Avanti. Bimbisara though different in ancestry was at least equal to the others in prowess and extent of kingdom. He committed Magadha to a career of conquest. The centripetal forces that began to operate under him stopped only at the time of Ashoka, when Magadha became the centre of an empire extending over India and Afghanistan.

Bimbisara was a great admirer of Buddha and his creed. In his old age he is said to have been imprisoned and killed by his son Ajatasatru (491-459 B.C.) who, however, later on submitted to the Buddha and became a convert to his creed. Fahien, the Chinese pilgrim, ascribes to him the foundation of new Rajgriha outside the hills and is partially supported by Hieun Tsiang. In the Pali text he is said to have repaired the fortifications of the city in anticipation of an attack from ferocious Pradyota, the king of Avanti.

Rajgriha was an important centre of Buddhism and the Buddha himself passed many years of his "ministration" at this place. It was the scene of many sermons and important events in his life. He lived in different localities of the city, but his favourite resort was Gridharkuta or the vultures' peak. He admired the city and its environments and his impression is summed up in his own words as given in the Pali text:

> "Delightful is Rajgriha, delightful is Gridharakuta, delightful is Gautama-nyagrodha, delightful is the Saptperin, cave on the side of Vaibhara, delightful is Kasia on the Rishigiri side, delightful is Sonpa-Saundika-Pragbhara in Sitavana, delightful is the Tapodarma, delightful is Kalandaka lake in Venuvan, delightful is the mangogrove of Jivaka, delightful is the deer park in Mardakukshi."

After the death of the Buddha, Ajatasatru brought his corporeal relics to Rajgir and enshrined them inside a stupa. A few months later when the leading Buddhist monks decided to hold a council to form a corpus of the teachings of the Buddha, Ajatasatru accommodated them in a large hall in front of the Sapt-parni cave, specially built for the purpose.

The modern religious importance for the place is largely due to Buddhism and Jainism which with a characteristic fondness for heights, have built temples at the top of almost all the hills. These temples throughout, laying claim to great antiquity, attract pilgrims from distant parts of India.

Rajgir is important for Muslims also because Hazrat Makhdoom Shah Sharfuddin Ahmed Aulia of Maner, the king of Salikas (a class of Faqirs) had made a special *Chilla* on the hill in the town of Rajgir, which may be described as the particular place of God. There is an *Idgah* just near the Laxmi Narayan Temple where *Namaz* is offered during *Id*.

Rajgir was under the Zamindari of Nawab of Hussainabad till the abolition of this system.

There are some folk shrines also in Rajgir where only local people worship.

With the passage of time different sect and sectarian shrines have also developed at Rajgir. Important among them are Anandamoyee Math, Ramakrishna Mission, Anand Marg, Arya Samaj and shrines of the Vaishnav sect.

Mythological account

In the Mahabharata Rajgir has been described as Karusha in the Magadh dynasty. The capital of Magadh during the Mahabharata war was Rajgir. A reference to Rajgir is also found in the ancient Hindu texts. The Rajgir Mahatam (Upadhyay, Yubraj N.D., p. 7) explains that while Ram and Laxman were on the way to Janakpur, they inquired about the place through which they were passing. Vishwamitra Muni told them :

> असूर्तर जसोनाम धर्मारण्यं महामतिः
> चक्रे पुरवरं राजा, वसुनीम गिरिव्रजमः

meaning thereby that the wisest Asurtrajas established Dharmarnya town and the king Basu established Grivraja town, which, in the course of time, was known as Rajgir. Similarly the same author expressing the religious importance of the place has mentioned that

> तच्छुत्वसेव पापेभ्योमुतः स्वलो कि माशुशः
> नरो राजगृहमं गच्छेत तीर्थसेवी जगद्धितः ।।६१।।
> उपस्य पृश्यततः स्मात्वा कक्षिवानि न मोदते
> वैभार विपुलश्चैव रत्नकूशे गिरव्रजः ।।६२।।
> रत्नाचलभिति रूयातः पचैते पावना नगा ।
> पञ्चानां शैले मुख्यानां मध्येशाले वराजते ।।६३।।

meaning thereby that Shiva, answering Parvati told her that if a pilgrim goes to Rajgir, he, by touching the water and bathing in the Kunds, would get Mahanand (eternal joy) and become free from all his past sins.

Buchanan's description

Buchanan, in his Patna-Gaya report of 1811-12 (1925), has mentioned that, "The fort was built by Raja Senok or Srinki and, being his residence, was called Rajgriha. The same person built Bargaon which is now known as Nalanda and was a contemporary of Mahavira. The first family of the king was Akwabongs of whom was Rikubdeo of Ayodhya, Sombongs of Hastinapuri. Srinki was one of these. An account of these families is contained in the Padmpuran and Adipuran—books belonging to the sect. Jarasandh was of Judobongs and Jain as were also Ram and Krishna and Shiva. They know nothing of the Buddhas. They claim the whole images of Shiva, Ganesh, Surya, etc., and all the hot springs, which they call by the same names with the Brahmans. They say that their images are known by both hands being joined in their lap, but on the same stone find the images with their hands in all positions." Further, he adds that he finds the remains of only two shrines, i.e. Maninag and Joradevi. He further says that the Brahman gave the same name to the five hills that the Jain but they do not consider them sacred.

Describing the Kshetra of the Kund he says, "Immediately west of the fort is a circular round containing a small cavity surrounded by a rampart of earth on which are some broken bricks. The Brahmins say that this was a math or abode built by a Dashaminand Gytanand, but this is quite absurd. A house could never have left such a ruin. He may have doubt upon it and some small temples of Siva. A small river which comes from the gap between the hills passes through the old ditch."

Some way up this torrent at a place called Sorswati in the passage between the two northern hills of the great range is a new ghat on each side of the torrent. Here is a dirty pool in the torrent which is considered holy by both Jain and Astik. Immediately over this ghat on the lower part of the hill to the west of the river is a collection of various springs and buildings, some of them old and some quite recent. The most celebrated is the Brahma Kund, a square cistern very deep and built partly with stone and partly with bricks. The water is collected in a pool at the bottom. An image of Ganesa is built into the wall. Below the Brahma Kund towards the east is a terrace to provide accommodation to religious mendicants of the Mela, on its south end is a small temple of Baraha with two Naginis somewhat different from those of Baragaon. Below the terrace is a square reservoir of bricks, containing five sacred springs which issue from an equal number of spouts made of stone, and the water, as it falls, is allowed to run off, so that it is perfectly clean, but where collected in the Kunds in which the people bathe, it is abominable.

Immediately south from the Brahma Kund and west from the temple of Varaha is a small temple of Shiva and extending the whole length of this temple and the Brahma Kund, on their west side is a long narrow reservoir built of bricks containing seven holy springs which issue from stone spouts, and the water is allowed to run off as it issues, except that a usual part is allowed to collect in puddles filled with frogs and other vermin and overwhelmed with weeds and rubbish. The first spring in this reservoir is named Gautam. The second is Bharadwaj and the third is Viswamitra Jamdagini, Durbasa and Parasasari, the fourth, fifth, sixth and seventh of these springs have become dry. In the wall of this place has been built an image of a Buddh or Jain, with both hands in the lap. It has a lotus flower on the soles of the feet and lions on the throne. It has a short inscription. In this cistern is lying a male figure somewhat like that usually called Vasudeva but somewhat different and notwithstanding its sex the Brahmins call it Devi or Goddess.

West to this reservoir are two small temples of Shiva and south from there is a reservoir containing a spout of stone which is the finest stream in the place. In the reservoir are lying two carved stones, one a Ganesh and the other a Buddha like figure. South of these is the Markanday Kund. In the reservoir are lying some images—a Gaurishankar, a male and a female standing, both called Devi with Buddha-like ears. On one side of the reservoir is a *darkhand* referred to as a temple of Kamaksha, but it contains no image. All these images except such as are objects of worship are said to have been brought from the hill above and the same has probably been the case with those which are worshipped, as they are in the same style and all resemble those at Bodh Gaya and Baragaon. The water from all these springs unites at the bottom of the hill and forms a stream rather larger than that at Sita Kund.

Describing Suraj Kund, Buchanan writes: "At the west end of the northern hill and east to the Brahm Kund is a cluster of springs and small temples similar to those opposite the Suraj Kund. This is a small reservoir in which the water is collected in a pool and does not form a spring so that it is beastly dirty and swarms with frogs. An image of Suraj, somewhat different from that at Kositirtha, is built in a wall and near it is a fat male figure with two arms and one leg heaving over the-throne. There is an inscription around it. This figure is in several other places intermixed with the Buddha and seems to bear resemblance to the cook of Gautama. In a small math of Shiva south-west from this kund is an image of the Buddha and on the outside are two throne-like stones. South from the Suraj Kund are two temples of Shiva with one Tulsi between them; one of them is called Halokeswar. South from there is the Sita Kund, the Ganesh Kund is north from there. Proceding from Suraj Kund somewhat east along the northern face of the hill is the Dargah of Sharfuddin Behari built where the great saint passed much of his time in prayer. The building although destitute of architectural merit is neat and clean and the area includes a hot spring formed into a pool called Sringeri Kund. Hindus are still permitted to bathe in the kund. During the Ramzan from eight to twelve hundred faithful assemble here and are entertained by the successors of the saint.

Buchanan has given a good account of the Kunds and shrines of Rajgir but he has failed to understand the basic tenets of Hinduism when he remarks that the Kunds are equally important for Hindus and Jains.

The Shrines 10

PRESENT SETTING

RAJGIR is a sacred town dominated by Upadhyas (Panda) in respect of economy and sacredness. Broadly, there are two sub-castes of Upadhyas, i.e. Yachak and Ayachak. Yachaks have the traditional and legal rights to carry on the profession of *Pandagiri* (priestcraft) whereas Ayachaks do not.

From the locational point of view the shrines of Rajgir can be devided into a Kund Zone and a Village Zone. The Kund Zone comprises shrines located in and around the kunds, two Buddhist temples, and shrines of Gupta Devi and Garh-mahadeva. The shrines of this zone are quite old and have been referred to in various scriptures. The rituals performed in this zone are of international and national level. Rituals performed during *Makar Mela* and *Malmas Mela* are also of great importance. In this zone the kunds of Rajgir have been referred to in many religious texts of different faiths. The village zone comprises shrines located in Rajgir village (now town), are recent in origin and are generally worshipped by the local people.

The following are the names of the shrines of the Kund Zone of Rajgir:

(1) Brahma Kund,
(2) Saptdhara,
(3) Panchmukhi Mahadwa,
(4) Laxhminarayan temple,
(5) Idgah,
(6) Nirmala sangat,
(7) Pipal tree,
(8) Upadhyaine temple,
(9) Daxinmaie temple,
(10) Vyas kund,
(11) Markanday kund,
(12) Kamakhya temple,
(13) Ganga-Jamuna kund
(14) Mahadeva temple on Vaibhargiri,
(15) Saptparni cave,

(16) Vishnupad temple,
(17) Joradevi temple,
(18) Sandhya Devi temple,
(19) Suraj Kund,
(20) Chandrama kund,
(21) Ganesh kund,
(22) Makhdoom kund,
(23) Dargah,
(24) Mosque,
(25) Karbala,
(26) Baitarni river,
(27) Dukhharinghat,
(28) Bharat kup,
(29) Shiva temple,
(30) Vishnu temple,
(31) Burmese temple,
(32) Japanese temple,
(33) Garhmahadeva,
(34) Guptamaie temple,
(35) Pipal tree,
(36) Nanak kund,
(37) Gurudwara,
(38) Maniyar Math,
(39) Gridhkutta,
(40) Santi stupa,
(41) Buddha's temple.

Hindu sacred centres of kund zone

Among the Hindu sacred centres of Rajgir kunds are considered as the most important sacred centres. Rajgir owes its importance as a place of pilgrimage to kunds. It is evident from the above list of shrines that trees, tanks, etc., have been also symbolized as sacred centres.

The main kunds of Rajgir are dedicated to seven rishis, namely, Bharadwaj, Bishwamitra, Yamdagini, Parshuram, Basistha, Kaushik and Atri. Hindus are the owners of these kunds and the Upadhyas of Rajgir the custodians. The kunds are largely maintained and repaired by these Upadhyas out of the offerings made by rich devotees. The most celebrated kund is the Brahma Kund. During my field work (1967-68) all the kunds except the Brahma Kund were dry. It is a hot kund and the water comes out naturally and spontaneously. There is an outlet in the kund to maintain the normal water level of the kund. In the western corner of the wall there is a stone idol of Brahma and Lakshmi where the devotees after bathing in the kund make the prescribed rituals with the assistance of the Upadhyas. Saptdhara is located at the eastern gate of the Brahma Kund. North to the Brahma Kund is the temple of Laxhminarayan. East to the Brahma Kund is the Anant Kund dedicated to lord Anant. The Vyas Kund is located east to the Anant Kund. During the various Melas it is popularly known as "ladies' Kund". Idols of Shiva, Laxmi and Narain are engraved in this kund. East of the Vyas Kund is the Markanday Kund. Northwest to the Vyas Kund is a temple enshrining the deities of Dhakshni Devi, Shiva and a pipal tree. These three are rotationally worshipped by the Upadhyas. A shrine, located north-east of the Laxhminarayan temple, has the idol of Balram, Shiva and Hanuman, and is locally known as Upadhyaine temple as it has been constructed by a female Upadhya. West to it is a pipal tree which is specially worshipped on Somwati Amawasya. South to the Brahma Kund is a Shiva temple. South-east to it is a Barhkshetra which is in a bad state of neglect. North-west to the Barhkshetra is the Nirmala Sangat, a Sikh sacred centre. On the extreme south of it is the Saraswati temple where a sadhu lives these days. West to the Nirmala Sangat is the Kashidhara. Below the Saraswati temple is the Saraswati.

All these sacred centres are at the foot of the Vaibhargiri. The shrines on the Vaibhargiri have Shiva, footprints of Vishnu, Joradevi and Sandhya Devi. Among these excepting Shiva all were in a state of neglect during the Makar Mela. East-south to the Brahma Kund is the Suraj Kund. It is under the foot of Vipulagiri. There are the Suraj Kund, Chanrma Kund and the Ram-Laxman Kund in one line. At a distance of one furlong in the same line there is another kund known as Sita Kund. The Ram-Laxman Kund is very dirty but the rest are quite clean. The Ram-Laxman Kund is known as such because the Great Ram and Laxman while passing this way during their exile washed their feet in this kund. Among these, the Suraj Kund is considered more important as a number of rituals are observed at this kund. South to the Sita Kund is an idol of the sun and Shiva. West to this kund is the Samadhi (grave) of Sommadutta (a Buddhist monk) where Buddhists usually perform some rituals. There is a Ganesh temple on the Vipulagiri but it remains neglected and is in ruins. A little away west from these kunds is the Baitarni river which remains completely neglected even during auspicious and festival days. There is a neglected Dhookh-harni ghat enshrining Dhookh Harini Maie. Close to it is the Saligram Kund enshrining the idol of Shiva. South to it is Bharatkupa enshrining an idol of Bharat. The room in which the idol was enshrined is now occupied by a watchman who lives in this room to keep a watch on the farms near by. These are the neglected shrines. There are two more Hindu sacred centres in the Kund Kshetra of Rajgir, i.e. Guptamaie and Garhmahdeva. The latter is in a condition of complete neglect and the former—a folk shrine in nature—is under the custody of a barber who managed to get the ownership of this shrine after winning a civil suit.

It is evident from the descriptions that the deities are represented through earthen or cemented lumps, engraved figures, paintings, trees, rivers, wells, tanks and kunds in the kund kshetra of Rajgir. The other striking feature of this kshetra is that though mythologically it remains a place of the activities of Krishna there is no shrine dedicated to him.

BUDDHIST SACRED CENTRES OF KUND ZONE

Buddhism, that wonderful teaching which declares life to be sorrow and yet is free from pessimism, which apparently inculcates the profoundest egoism and yet is extolled for the loftiest morality which denies the "I" the soul and yet teaches absolute responsibility for deeds through rebirth which is without God or prayer and yet offers the most certain salvation. This wonderful teaching was propounded by Gautam of the aristocratic Sakya clan. The new current which the Buddha started within the Indian culture has ultimately become an essential part of world culture as a whole. The basic moral and spiritual ideas which the Buddha preached had carried forward a certain ancient religious and cultural tradition and become in turn the source of a manifold development which expressed itself in the setting up of a high and refined moral ideal, promoting charitable activities. The rich stream of cultural life inspired by the Buddha progressed during the centuries following his Parinirvan, gradually acquiring a varied and individual aspect but ever remaining a tributary of that large stream of Indian culture into which it ultimately merged. The Buddha's teachings differed according to the intellectual level of his audience and the Pali canon contains many later developments.

Magadh has been the craddle of Buddhism and in this territory the religion continued to flourish till the last when it was wiped away by the arms of Islam. The most famous centres of Buddhism lay in ancient Magadh or modern Bihar, viz. Bodh Gaya, Rajgir, Nalanda and Vaishali. Rajgir in northern India is one of the important sacred places of Buddhism. Bimbisara and Ajatasatru were in personal touch with the Buddha and paid him the homage due from pupils. The Buddha had spent much of his time in preaching at Rajgir where laymen and monks had formed themselves into communities. The first council of monks had been held and the compilation of the canons was done at Rajgir after six months of Parinirvana with five hundred monks.

After the passing away of the Buddha there arose great controversies among his followers with regard to the interpretation of the teacher and also about the rules of discipline. The latter resulted in the two sects of Buddhism, that is, Hinyan and Mahayan. We find the representation of both the sects at Rajgir. Thus the two well-known historical divisions into which Buddhism was cut are the Hinyan, which means little vehicle, and the Mahayan which means the great vehicle. Hinyan stands for ancient Buddhism while Mahayan stands for developed Buddhism. Rajgir is an important centre of Buddhism where Buddha himself passed years of his ministration. It was the scene of many sermons and important events of his life. He lived in the different localities of the city but his favourite resort was the Gridhakutta. He admired the city and its environments. All the sacred centres of Buddhism fall within the kund kshetra.

Fa-hien the Chinese pilgrim who visited Rajgir in the 5th century found the valley desolate and a band of monks inhabiting the monastery of the Venuvan. Hieun Tsiang, another famous Chinese pilgrim, visited Rajgir in the second quarter of the 7th century. He could not say much about the contemporary condition of a place because he found it deserted.

Burmese and Japanese Buddhist sacred centres

At present the sacred centre of the Hinyan sect is locally known as Burmese Buddhist temple. It was constructed in 1935 by Lt. Kundernmaya. Ven. Z. Zayanata is the chief priest of this temple. His disciples are his brother's and sister's sons. A marble idol of the Buddha is centrally located in the sanctum and it has been tastefully decorated.

The sacred centre of the Mahayan sect is locally known as Japanese Buddhist temple. It was constructed by Sri Nichidatusa Fujijee in 1928. A Japanese idol is centrally placed in the sanctum located in upper storey of the building. Another important Buddhist sacred centre is the Venuvan. It is said that the Buddha stayed in the Venuvan for a long period. In the Pali text it has been referred to as Kalanda Nivapa. Two idols of the Buddha have been enshrined in the Venuvan. Another sacred centre is Somdutta's Samadhi. It is a neglected shrine and people were seen cooking food on this samadhi. A few more sacred centres are located on the Gridhakutta. The Gridhakutta is considered sacred because Buddha spent many days on it. At the top of the hill there is a platform where Buddha used to sit. There is a stupa on the Gridhakutta being reconstructed by the Mahayan sect of Rajgir. South to this stupa is the shrine of the Buddha. Another Buddhist sacred centre is the Pipal stone house and Saptparin cave on the Vaibhar hill.

Sikh sacred centres

Rajgir is not that important for the followers of the Sikhism as it is for the followers of Hinduism, Buddhism, Jainism and Islam. Bihar cannot be called the home of Sikhism but since the great patriot-saint Guru Govind Singh who was born in 1664 in Patna, it is considered as one of the holy places of Sikhism. Though he seems to have been a Guru of the Sikhs, he was, in fact, the hope of Hindu India of those days and it was he who inspired people with the hope that they could revive if they would unite and fight. Perhaps, the greatest achievement of Guru Govind Singh was his declaration that the mission of the Gurus had ended with him and that the Sikhs in future were to seek the guidance of God only in the collective voice of the community and in the sacred writings of the Ten Gurus. Thus the community became self-contained and the devoted followers of the teachings of Nanak and the nine Gurus that followed him have immense influence on the Sikhs.

Once Nanak Saheb passed through Rajgir and addressed a public meeting at which his devotees requested him for a cold water kund. According to the request of his devotees he turned a hot water Naiekund into a cold water kund. This Naiekund, in course of time, became Nanak Kund. Nirmala Sangat is another Sikh sacred centre located north-east of Brahm Kund. It is said that a Sikh lady came here in 1830 from Punjab at the age of eighteen and started living on the kund. Bholanath Panda was the first among the Pandas to be influenced by her mystic activities. Later, Pandas gave her food, shelter and accommodated her in Upadhya-toli—the residential locality of the Pandas. Thus she could establish a Sangat known as Nirmala Sangat but none of the local people could join her faith. On her death, Badho Upadhya became the chief of the Sangat. The Sangat is in a completely dilapidated condition today.

A temporary Gurudwara was constructed in front of the Nanak Kund in 1965. Till 1964 it was known as Naie Kund and the Naies of Rajgir were its custodians. All Mundans (hair-shaving ceremony) were performed at this kund. But in December, 1964, few members of the Singh Sabha of the Patna came and forcibly occupied it. A title suit is pending in the Patna High Court on behalf of the Naies (barbers) of Rajgir. These days Mundans are performed at the Saraswati Kund. Currently there are two *Paiejees* in this Gurudwara.

Muslim sacred centres of Kund Kshetra

The Muslim immigrants who settled in Bihar and became part of its population had certain distinctive features. Their cardinal doctrine was unity of God. Islam admitted of no compromise even for illustration or artistic purposes. They believed in congregational worship and prayers which focus a sense of solidarity among them. Islam is a missionary religion without a missionary organization. There are two sects of Islam. i.e. Shia and Sunni. Apart from the doctrine of Immamat the difference between the Sunnite and the Shiite Schools is not very great.

THE IDGAH

Rajgir was under the rule of a Nawab for a considerable span of time. The Idgah is an important sacred centre of the Kund Zone. It is located in front of the stairs leading to the Brahm

Kund. There is another neglected sacred centre in this zone on the Pipla stone house of Vaibhar hill. On the top of the structure are five Muslim graves (four on a brick platform in the centre and one to the south of it). Another sacred centre of this zone is Makhdoom Kund. It was previously a Hindu kund known by the name of Srivangrishi Kund. But after a court decision regarding the right over the kund it was transferred to Muslims and since then it is known as Makhdoom Kund named after a saint, Hazrat Makhdoom Shah Sharfuddin Ahmed. The twin-dhara was previously known as Ram and Laxman Dhara but now has no name. The present *chilla* above the kund was earlier the shrine of Ram, Laxman and Sita.

Fairs and the sacred centres

A religious fair is held at the foot of the Vaibhargiri Hill on the occasion of Malmas (intercalary month). It took place during the intercalary month which falls after every three years. Pilgrims come from different parts of the country believing that by taking a bath in the kund one washes off all his sins. It is believed that a bath in the kund and prayers to all Gods and deities of the Kund Zone would purify a sinner. Pilgrims offer rich gifts to the Pandas.

Another religious fair is Makarmela beginning from the first day of Magh. Pilgrims from different regions come to have a holy dip in the kund. They give alms to beggars after taking a holy dip. A religious fair is also held at the Vaibhargiri hill and on the kunds on the occasion of Shivaratri—a day devoted to the worship of Lord Shiva and his consort Parvati. Shivaratri is held on the fourteenth of the dark half of Phalgun and is believed in Rajgir as elsewhere to be the night of Shiva's marriage with Parvati. On this occasion a crowd is seen on the hill shrines during the afternoon of Shivaratri from late evening until late in the night. In addition to the locals some pilgrims from distant places also come to join in the worship. The kund is also visited on several sacred days and months according to the Hindu calendar for a holy dip and other rituals. The Suraj Kund also provides a place for sun worship. The kund is regionally known as a place for special bath on Kartik Purnima. Similarly on the occasion of an eclipse a crowd of thousands on the regional scale assembles to bathe in the kund. Moreover the kunds are universally known as a place of pilgrimage to earn merit in this life and also in the heavens throughout the Hindu world.

Essence of Indian civilization

The Buddhist sacred centres which were of high importance during the past several centuries are today in the declining phase at Rajgir. Rajgir, which has witnessed the birth of Buddhism, is today witnessing the mordern trend of Buddhism. Though Rajgir has international patronage Buddhism is yet to be revitalized. Similar is the case with Jainism. Sikhism and Islam which never had any strong footing at Rajgir have now become a strong base for these two sects. In the case of Hindu sacred centres, the old shrines are in a dilapidated condition—a few are being remodelled but Rajgir has definitely become a good ground for the shrines/ashrams of modern religious intellectuals like Ramakrishna Mission, Anandmie, etc.

It is evident from the foregoing that the sacred centres are found in close proximity with each other irrespective of any sectarian consideration. This suggests the essence of Indian civilization, i.e. unity in diversity at micro level, at Rajgir. This can be illustrated with several examples, i.e. location of Somdatt's Samadhi and Suraj Kund, etc.

Pilgrims visiting Rajgir do come with different motives. Hundreds such pilgrims who visited Rajgir during the Makar Mela were interviewed to know the specific purpose of their visit. Fiftyfive of them did not give any specific answer. Twenty-nine of them disclosed their purpose as the fulfilment of mundane desires for which vows had been taken or were to be taken. Sixteen of them said that they had come to earn merit in the next life. The following table gives an agewise clear picture of the motives for visiting Rajgir:

	Purpose of visit		
Age group	Recreation	To enjoy hot spring and accidental worship	To earn merit in this or next life/ Religiosity
0-20 years	80%	12%	8%
21-40 years	60%	30%	10%
41-60 years	45%	25%	30%
60 onwards	10%	30%	60%

In the above table by accidental worship is meant that those who come to enjoy the hot springs also perform various rituals at different sacred centres of the kund zone of Rajgir on the persuasion of the Pandas of Rajgir.

It has been mentioned earlier that some shrines belonging to different sectoral groups are in a dilapidated condition and are not visited by the pilgrims of the respective sects. It has also been found here that a few new shrines of different sectoral groups have been constructed by the generous devotees of the respective sects. Buchanan has mentioned about twentyseven shrines in his report whereas Rajgir Mahants mention fiftyfive shrines which are currently located at Rajgir.

Shrines of village zone

The Village Zone is located at a distance of about 2 km from the Kund Zone. It is being termed as Village Zone because the entire area of this zone was inhabited by the Upadhyas (Pandas) of Rajgir. They call this area as their village. In course of time important shrines of different sects were constructed in this zone. The shrines of this zone have not been referred to in any text. Travellers like Fahien and Hieun Tsiang and Buchanan have not made any reference to any shrines while mentioning the life of villagers in their report. The Village Zone is the stronghold of Jainism in comparison to Hinduism, Sikhism, Buddhism or Islam.

Hindu shrines

There is a Mayadevi temple in the Upadhyatoli. She is the Kuldevi of the Pandas of Rajgir. Besides her is an idol of Lord Shiva too. Only Upadhyas are allowed to perform rituals in this shrine. At a distance of a hundred yards west of Mayadevi temple is the temple of Lord Krishna locally known as Banshidhar Thakurbari constructed by Pandit Jaggarnath Panda in 1938. Fifty yards west to this is another shrine of the Snakes God known as Nagmandir. This temple came into light when an Upadhya was getting plinth work done for the construction of his house. It is said that when the spade touched the Snake God the place was full of snakes. The snakes disappeared only when the Upadhya offered milk. The Anandmaie Math is also located at a short distance from here. It is an international *math* registered with the U.P. Government and established by a widow. North-west to the Anandmaie Math is the temple of Laxmi Narayan. It was constructed in 1962 to fill the gap of a shrine of Vaishnava sect by Sri Madhusudanacharyajee. About a furlong south to this temple is the Kalibari managed by Bhavtarni Banprastha Ashram. There is a Ramakrishna Mission located fifty yards west of the Laxmi Narayan temple. In the market, the oldest shrine of this zone, i.e. Udasin Sangat, is located where the idol of Srichand is worshipped by his followers. South-east to it is the sacred centre of the Arya Samaj.

There is no Sikh sacred centre in this zone. There is also no Buddhist sacred centre in this zone.

Muslim sacred centre

In the Village Zone there are two mosques in which one, Barimilki, located in Gwala-toli, is in a dilapidated condition. The other mosque is also located in Gwala-toli where a Maulvi offers Namaz occasionally.

Sacred performances

The Laukik and textual rituals are performed at various shrines of Rajgir. Such rituals may be performed on a ground or small level depending upon the economic condition and religious mental make-up of the pilgrim or citizen. Rituals, performed at different levels at Rajgir, are discussed here.

A worshipper at all the Hindu shrines of Rajgir makes offerings of water, flowers, leaves, fruits and a few grains of Arwa rice like at other places of Hindu pilgrimage world. After bathing in the kund a worshipper offers flowers and the kund's holy water to the deity engraved in the wall of the kund. Sometime camphor is also waved before it and some money are given to the Panda as *Dan* (gift). Thereafter pilgrims/citizens go to the different shrines according to Tithi (date) and one's own choice.

The Upadhyas perform rituals daily in rotation believing that the deities are being worshipped traditionally by them. Among them are the Brahm Kund, Suraj Kund, Daxhini Devi's temple, the shrine of Baba Bhootnath, Barahkhetra and Maya Devi's temple. Each adult Upadhya worships all these temples in rotation. These shrines are strictly worshipped in rotation by the Yachak Upadhyas only.

Prarthana, Paath, Jap and Dhyan are yet another kind of sacred performance done at Rajgir by the pilgrims or citizens. Pilgrims/citizens sing Prarthana after taking a bath in the kund and do Paath (recitation of sacred texts) at various shrines. Another important ritual is performed during the Makar Mela. Pilgrims from distant places come here to take a holy dip. Textually it is believed that a dip in the kund of Rajgir washes off all the sins of an individual. Textually, one is advised to bathe in the kunds of Rajgir in the following order:

(1) Saraswati Kund
(2) Ram Laxman Kund
(3) Ganesh Kund,
(4) Chandrama Kund,
(5) Sita Kund
(6) Suraj Kund,
(7) Markandey Kund,
(8) Vyas Kund,
(9) Anant Kund,
(10) Ganga Kund,
(11) Saptdhara Kund,
(12) Brahma Kund,
(13) Vaitarni river,
(14) Dhookh Harnighat,
(15) Saligram Kund,
(16) Bharat Kund.

However, no citizen or pilgrim observes this order. Maybe because some of the kunds are dry or because of the lack of textual knowledge of the pilgrims/citizens and also of the Pandas who are considered as the custodians of the kunds of Rajgir.

Elaborate rituals are performed by the pilgrims/citizens on the occasion of Sombati Amawasya. Girls also do it in the belief that they would get good husbands without causing much problem to their parents. Married women do it for the welfare of their husbands. On the occasion of Nagpanchami, the Naag (of the Village Zone) is offered milk and Lawa (fried rice). Sometimes a *been* (a musical instrument) is also played to please the snake deity at the local *Nag* shrine. Performance of music by an individual is only marked during Nagpanchami and Janmasthami.

Coming to the Buddhist sacred performances we note that the different rituals performed by the Buddhists are known as self-examination. They are observed from 7 December to 31

December. During self-examination a fast is observed. In the morning they go to Gridhkutta and return from there late in the night. They beat the drum and sing hymns for ten hours in a day; in the morning they see the risingsun. Fruther it is clear from the name of the sacred performance that they examine themselves to know whether they are able to maintain their sacredness or not. This all has been prescribed for the priests with a view to keeping them always pure and in the belief that by observing this performance they would be able to maintain their sacredness.

Coming to the Sikh sacred performance it has been observed that on the occasion of Guru Nanak's birthday and on the first day of Baisakh a procession originates from the Nanak temple and terminates at the Nanak Kund after moving through the town. Pilgrims from adjoining cities come to participate in the ritual.

Similarly, Muslims also offer Namaz at their sacred centres on the festive days. It has been mentioned earlier that a Maulvi offers Namaz regularly at the Makhdoom Kund and other sacred centres five times a day. At all the Hindu shrines of Rajgir also, the priests perform some rituals regularly in the early morning, noon, evening and night. In the Hinyan Buddhist shrines of Rajgir the regular sacred performance is observed thrice in a day which they call Sikho, Nimat Sikho and Puzawa. They offer flowers, Mala and Dhoop while performing the ritual and chant:

नभोत्स: भगवतो अरह्तो समासम बुद्यो
बुद्योपदोन आम धर्मोपदना नमाभी
संघोपदो नमाभी

meaning, "O Lord Buddha, you are great, I bow my head in your prayer and I bow my head in the name of the Sangha". It is a significant mantra because they spell it before observing any sacred performance. In the Mahayan shrines of Rajgir, regular rituals are performed thrice a day by ringing of bells and beating of the drum accompanied by the chanting of the following mantra:

नम् म्योहो रेंगो क्यों ;

They go to the Gridh Kutta to perform the regular noon rituals.

The Sacred Specialists 11

THE SACRED shrines and the rituals performed at Rajgir have been discussed in the preceding pages. Pilgrims or citizens who desire to perform rituals require assistance and guidance. A particular group of persons is always found at different kunds for this purpose. There is the other class of persons who remains associated with the shrines of Rajgir and performs regular rituals there. At some shrines a devotee/pilgrim has to strictly go through the priests for offering any ritual article to the deity. The persons who assist pilgrims/citizens in the performing of rituals at Rajgir are known as Sacred Specialists because they have the specialized knowledge of Laukik and Shastrik rituals and fully depend on the profession of priestcraft for their livelihood. They can be classified according to their level of knowledge, level of participation in the ritual, mode of interaction with the pilgrims/citizens, Jati-Upjati composition and sectorial composition. For analytical convenience, they are being described here on the sectorial basis.

HINDU

Upadhyas are the most important sacred specialists of Rajgir. They fully depend on the profession of prietscraft for their livelihood. They are considered the custodians of the kunds of Rajgir. They are popularly known as Pandajee. The social and cultural element of the Upadhyas unites them into a single caste. Regarding their origin at Rajgir, the *Rajgir Mahatam* says that there was a king named Basunam who once wanted to perform a *yag*. He was in need of a few scholarly Pandits for this. So he invited the Upadhyas. With them some uninvited Upadhyas also came who, in course of time, came to be known as Ayachak Upadhyas. The *Rajgir Mahatam* further tells that 7,500 Upadhyas came from Dravida, Maharashtra, Karnataka, Kokan and Tamil Nadu belonging to the following fourteen Gotras:

(1) Wats,	(8) Bhardwaj,
(2) Upnaan,	(9) Kausik,
(3) Kautilya,	(10) Kashyap,
(4) Garg,	(11) Basistha,
(5) Harit,	(12) Parasar,
(6) Gotam,	(13) Saraswati,
(7) Sandilya,	(14) Punarwasa.

Both invited and uninvited, Yachak and Ayachak, belong to the above fourteen Gotras. King Basunam did not ask the uninvited Upadhyas to go back since the Brahmins were enjoying a superior position in society, rather the uninvited were requested by King Basunam to help and assist the invited Upadhyas (Yachak Upadhyas) in assisting and guiding the pilgrims in performing the numerous laukik and shastrik rituals at the kunds of Rajgir. The Ayachaks were given land to settle themselves. Thus from that day, Ayachaks do not directly offer their services to pilgrims in the performing of rituals but they simply assist Yachak Upadhyas.

Yachak Upadhyas are the custodian of the kunds and all other Hindu sacred centres of the Kund Zone of Rajgir. They assist and guide pilgrims during Malmas and Makar Mela and on other occasions. They have a rich knowledge of Laukik and Shastrik rituals. Some of them are also well-versed in Sanskrit. All Yachak Upadhyas live at one place, i.e. in Panda-toli and have a uniform residential pattern. Panda-toli is located in the heart of Rajgir town. A few shrines are also located in the Upadhya-toli. A few Upadhyas also live in the nearby villages. They come to the kunds to assist and guide pilgrims only on the occasion days. The Upadhyas, in general, speak the Maghi dialect with an accent of their own which is known as Pandaboli. The traditional or ceremonial dress of the Upadhyas is Kurta, Dhoti, Pagri and a Chaddar on the shoulder but their usual dress in half-shirt and dhoti.

They have joint family system. A such family consists of male members of two or three generations and the unmarried daughters living in the same family. They have close relationship with their paternal and maternal relatives due to local endogamy. They share in each other's joys and sorrows. A child after having Upnayan Sanskar usually begins his career of *Pandagiri*. He does not assist and guide the pilgrims independently but works as a junior for sometime to learn the art of the profession. Children usually consider their parents as Gods and respect their elders. An orthodox Upadhya does not take food even if prepared by a respectable Brahmin. He eats only that food which has been prepared by a male or female Upadhya or by himself. Upadhyas are strictly vegetarian and teetotaller but it has now been reported that a few of them have become non-vegetarian and also take liquor.

Women respect their husbands and consider them next to God. Widow marriage is not allowed. It is said that before marriage a woman is under the control of her father and after marriage under the control of her husband's father, husband and sons.

There are two important phases of Upadhya life—Yagopawit and Vivah. Yagopwit is performed between the age of seven and nine. Until it is performed Yachak Upadhyas usually do not allow their sons to assist and guide a pilgrim or citizen in the performing of rituals at the kunds of Rajgir. The second important phase is Vivah or marriage. No Upadhya is allowed to perform any ritual at family-level until he himself is married.

An Upadhya tries to be relieved from the duties of a Panda as soon as his son/sons become able to take charge of the profession. When so free he devotes more of his time to religious activities for his own benefit and less for the benefit of his Yajmans. It is believed that attainment of Moksha or going to heaven or hell depends on one's own Karma.

The daily life of an Upadhya depicts him as a religious man and devoted to the profession of priestcraft. He leaves his bed in the early morning uttering the name of his favourite God and sings bhajan (religious song). He goes to the kund to have a bath and to worship the deities of his own. He assists and guides the pilgrims till 11 a.m. or so depending on the number the pilgrims. He returns home to take food. He is strictly vegetarian. He then relaxes and also discussses family affairs with other family members. Then he goes to the kund, usually at 4 p.m., to assist and guide pilgrims and remains here till 7 p.m. He returns home after performing the Sandhya Arti at different shrines and at the kunds of Rajgir. He also take Bhaang while moving around the shrines of Rajgir. Usually, he retires for the day at 8.30 p.m. after performing Annapurna Pujan and then taking dinner.

Upadhyas visit their Jajmans during the off season. They not only believe in taking Daan (gift) but also in giving Daan to the poor with a view to earning merit. Any result is considered either as boon or curse of the God. Their such beliefs stimulate them to become more ritualistic. Old Upadhya women are also regular visitors to the Kund and the shrines located in the Kund Zone. Young women usually worship at the shrines located within the village and occasionally at the shrines of the Village Zone. The eldest woman of the family is made responsible for the worship by the family at the traditional shrines of the Kund and Village Zone. An Upadhya woman is working as the custodian of the Ladies Kund. She has been made the custodian since there is no male member in her family to look after her and other members of the family.

Ayachak Upadhyas are not the custodians of the Kund. They are functionally simply assistants of the Yachak Upadhyas and are paid for their services. In almost all Jain shrines Ayachak Upadhyas are working as priests on a monthly salary but they have not become Jain. A few Ayachak Upadhyas have also adopted independent professions like practice of homoeopathy, business, etc. If an Ayachak Upadhya marries a Yachak Upadhya girl and if the girl has no brother then he inherits the share of Yachak Upadhya as sacred specialist. These two subcastes marry into each other. The total population of the Upadhyas is 400. It is said that their number is declining. Endogamy is considered to be the cause for this. Upadhyas are interested in having matrimonial connections outside Rajgir but have yet to achieve any success.

The changes occurring in the community at present are considered harmful to the cause of Hindu tradition. They are very much conscious of the profession of priestcraft and still wish to stick to their traditional profession.

Apart from Upadhyas, Gwalas (milkmen), Naies (barbers),

Malis (garland makers) are also working as priests of different shrines of Rajgir. A few places named after religious intellectuals like Anandmaie, Ramkrishna, etc., have also been found at Rajgir.

BUDDHIST

Hinyan and Mahayan, the two sects of Buddhism, have their own sacred specialists. There is only one sacred specialist in the Buddhist Hinyan sacred centre of Rajgir. The sacred specialist is locally known as Bhiksu and a Bhiksu, by definition, is a "beggar" living on alms, having no permanent abode. To become Bhiksu the first stage is of sermon in which one eats only once during the day. And it is all up to the Guru to test him and, if found fit, to declare him a Bhiksu in course of time. There is no time limit for this. A Bhiksu's main moto is to attain Nirvana.

There are five sacred specialists of the Mahayan Buddhist sect at Rajgir. Of them four are Japanese and one a South Indian. The services of these priests are transferrable. They are not permitted to marry. They are vegetarian and their main moto of life is to attain Nirvana and to work for the welfare of the community.

SIKH

There are two Sikh sacred specialists in the gurdwara of the Nanak Kund. They are known as Paiejee. They are not permitted to marry. They are not locals, they are from Patna city.

MUSLIM

There is a Maulvi at the Makhdoom Kund. His day-to-day expenses are met by those who stay at the Kund. He is here on his own.

Conclusion 12

From the foregoing, it is fairly clear that the Gaya model of a sacred complex (Vidyarthi, 1961) is widely applicable to Rajgir and also perhaps to all the Puranic tirthas of India. This is generally because the three elements which constitute the structure of a sacred complex, i.e. sacred geography, sacred performances and sacred specialists are there and are upheld by pilgrims of all categories.

The sacred complex of Rajgir represents in a microcosm the Indian civilization, that is to say, the sacred complex of Rajgir represents unity in diversity. There are various sacred centres belonging to various sects but the cult of kund predominates noticeably. The sacred centres belonging to Buddhism, Jainism, Sikhism and Islam have their sacred centres but somehow or other they also are associated with the kunds. They observe their own festivals and perform their own rituals but the kund has some role in all these. The degree of association with the kund may vary from one sect to another.

There is homogeneity among the sacred specialists of Rajgir at the macro level in spite of the fact that they are not only of different castes but also belong to different sects. The Brahminical and non-Brahminical specialists represent here the great and little traditions respectively. The sacred specialists belonging to Buddhism, Jainism, Sikhism and Islam are non-Brahminical but represent the great tradition. Some of the non-Brahminical specialists belonging to Hinduism are basically oriented in the little tradition but operate with the specialists of the great tradition.

The sacred complex of Rajgir unites not only the Hindus all over the world but also people of different nations belonging to different sects. Pilgrims from Japan, Ceylon, Thailand,

Nepal, Bangladesh, Pakistan and other countries belonging to Buddhism, Jainism, Sikhism and Islam lead the same life as Indian pilgrims in Rajgir.

Pilgrims from different national, political, social and economic groups belonging to different sects who worship at the kunds of Rajgir identify themselves with kund owing to its association with the Gurus of the respective sects and share in common most of the sacred performances at kunds as prescribed by the sacred tradition of Rajgir and also share the common cultural knowledge transmitted by their repective sacred specialists.

The sacred complex of Rajgir provides an opportunity for the pilgrims of different nations, sects and castes to interact with each other and lead a common life. However, they do discriminate among themselves at microlevel but, at macro level they are closer.

The sacred specialists of Rajgir belonging to different sects broadly maintain a distinct style of life at macro level but, at micro level, have heterogenous style.

The nature of sacred in the Hindu cultural tradition is not as simple as one finds in the Semitic culture. In both Christianity and Islam the descent of man on earth is itself proof of his sin and the expiation of this sin is his ultimate goal for which he must regain the sacred, the paradise which he has lost. Therefore, secular is synonymous with profane, and the logical antithesis of the sacred. But in the Brahminic, Buddhist, Sikh and Jain sacred tradition man is not a despised being; he is not inherently subservient to God. This aspect of the sacred complex of Rajgir makes it distinct from other sacred complexes.

The places which are of sacred importance are also of secular importance. A place of sacred nature for one sect may be of secular for another. It is obvious that sacred is more or less used as a tool in the various spheres of man's activity, and for achieving his earthly goal a pilgrim or citizen irrespective of his sect or nation seems to have no inhibitions whatsoever. In the circumstances, in the background of Indian cultural traditions, one fails to put "sacred" and "secular" into two water-tight compartments. In the drudgery of social life one may find certain diacritical marks artificially dividing people into high and low, but as one comes to a place like Rajgir, this difference begins to evaporate.

A sacred complex, it can be argued, serves as both a place as well as a cause for national integration in a country like India known for its diversity. The institution of pilgrimage is perhaps even more effective as a means of integration because of improved means of transport and communication.

Select Bibliography

Apte, V.M., Religon and philosophy in R.C. Majumdar (ed.) *The Vedic Age*, London, 1951.

Allen, Graut, *The evolution of the idea of God*, 1949.

Bary, W.T., *Sources of Indian tradition*, 1958.

Bannett, L.D., *Antiquities of India*, London, 1913.

Benton, M., *Anthropological approaches to the study of Indian Religion*, 1960.

Basu, R.N., *History of Ancient India.*

Bandarkar, R.G., *Vaishnavism, Saivism and minor religious systems*, Strassburg, 1913.

Bhargava, M.L., *The Geography of Rigvedic India*, Lucknow, 1964.

Bose, N.K., *Cultural Anthropology and other essays*, Calcutta, 1953.

Brown, P., *Indian Architecture*, Bombay, 1948.

Buchanan, H., District Report, 1812.

Burgees, J.J., *Geography of India*, Indian Antiquities, Vol. XX, 1891.

Cambess, J., Myth and Symbol in Indian Art and Civilization.

Chaudhary, R.G.S., *Rambles in Bihar*, Patna, 1917.

Cunningham, A., *Ancient Geography of India*, 1871.

Gillin, J., *Religion and Modern Society*, 1964.

Deissman, A., *A Study in Social and Religious History*, 1927.

Dikshitar, V.R. Ramchandra, *The Purana Index*, Madras.

Dubey, S.C., *Indian Village*, Cornell University Press, 1955.

Durkheim, E., *The Elementary form of Religious life*, 1915.

Fa-Haien, *Travels of Fa-Haien* Translated by H.A. Gilles, 1923.

Fuchs, Stephen, *The Children of Hari*, Bombay, 1960.

Ghurye, G.S., *Indian Sadhu*, Bombay, 1953.

Harper, E.B., *Religion in South Asia*, 1964.

Hunter, W.W., *Annals of Rural Bengal.*

Jha, M., *Sacred Complex in Janakpur*, Allahabad, 1971.

Kare, P.V., *History of Hindu Dharma Sastra*, Vol. 3, Poona, 1930.

Lewis, Oscar, Peasant culture in India and Mexico, in Mekim Marriott (ed.) *Village India*, Chicago, 1955.

——, The Jajman system in a North India village, *Scientific monthly*, Vol. 83, No. 2, 1956.

Mansfield, P.T., *Bihar Orissa in 1930-31.*

Majumdar, D.N., *Caste and Communication in an Indian Village*, Bombay, 1958.

Mukherjee, Radhakumud, *Nationalism in Hindu Culture.*

Moor, Edward, *Plates Illustrating the Hindu Panthion*, 1861.

Mukherjee, D.P., *Modern Indian Culture*, Bombay, 1948.

O'Malley, L.S.S., Indian caste customs, 1932, *Santhal Pargana District Gazetteers*, 1938.

Pande, R.B., *Hindu Sanskars: A Socio-religious Study of Hindu Sacraments*, 1949.

Pannikkar, K.K., *Hindu Society at Cross-roads*, 1967.

Puran, *Shiva Puran*, N.D.

Rajpuri, A.B., *Basukinath Mahatam*, N.D.

Redfield, Robert, *The Little Community*, Chicago, 1955.

Redfield, Robert, and Milton Singer, The Cultural role of Cities, *Man in India*, Vol. 36, No. 3, 1965.

Saraswati, B.N., The Holy circuit of Niwsar, *Journal of Social Research*, Vol. 8, No. 2, 1965.

Sinha, Surjit, Tribal culture of Peninsular India as a dimension of little tradition in the study of Indian civilization: A preliminary statement, *Man in India*, Vol. 37, No. 2.

Singer, Milton, The Cultural pattern of Indian civilization : A preliminary report of a methodological field study, *The Far Eastern Quarterly*, Vol. 15, No. 1, 1955. The Great Tradition in a Metropolitan Centre: Madras in Traditional India, Structure and change (ed.), *Journal of American Folklore*, Vol. 71, No. 281.

Vidyarthi, L.P., Thinking about a sacred city, *The Eastern Anthropologist*, Vol. 13, No. 1, 1980; *The Sacred Complex in Hindu Gaya*, Concept Publishing Company, New Delhi, 1980, 1961.

Vidyarthi, L.P. (ed.), Aspects of Religion in Indian Society Meerut, 1962.

Wayman, A., The twenty one praises of Tora, *Journal of Bihar Research Society*, 1961.

Wilson, Braya R., *Sects and Society*, 1961.

Annual Report of—Balanand Brahmachari Ashram, *Deosangh Ashram Satsang Ashram Sri Sri Jugal Mandir*.

INDEX